KV-637-810

SCIENCE AND ENGINEERING POLICY SERIES

General Editors Sir Harrie Massey
Sir Frederick Dainton

Computers, Communications and Society

MURRAY LAVER

OXFORD UNIVERSITY PRESS 1975

Oxford University Press, *Ely House, London W.1*

Glasgow	Bombay
New York	Calcutta
Toronto	Madras
Melbourne	Karachi
Wellington	Lahore
Cape Town	Decca
Salisbury	Kuala Lumpur
Ibadan	Singapore
Nairobi	Hong Kong
Dar es Salaam	Toyko
Lusaka	
Addis Ababa	

ISBN 0 19 858323 0

©OXFORD UNIVERSITY PRESS 1975

Reproduced and printed by photolithography and bound in
Great Britain at The Pitman Press, Bath

Preface

It has become fashionable to bewail the adverse effects which the continued complication of technology is having on the quality of our lives, and to discount the benefits that it is intended to produce. The broader questions of policy which are raised are not ones that technologists have any specific competence to answer. Their skills are more narrowly, but quite properly, directed at increasing the efficiency of the means employed rather than at improving the choice of the ends to be sought, or assessing the consequences for society. This is not to say that no expert has a conscience: most, indeed, share their profession's sense of public responsibility; nevertheless, the fundamental social and political questions cannot be shuffled off on to them; they concern each one of us, as individuals and as electors, and we need to be able to participate effectively in their discussion. In no branch of technology is this more important than in telecommunications and computing, for these provide essential information services that we use in all our affairs—economic, social, and political. Moreover, the time is uniquely right, for we are poised at the beginning of what may well prove to be the most significant technical change of the last hundred years: the combination of computing and telecommunications. This field is a specialized one, and it is surrounded by an aura of mystery; but it not so esoteric that the examination of its broader implications lies beyond the layman's reach. This book is intended to contribute to the information of non-specialists so that a general discussion of these important matters can begin.

Sidmouth, Devon   F.J.M.L.
May 1974

Contents

Seven times a second

When Galileo turned his telescope towards the moon and the planets he
set astronomy on an entirely fresh course and provided one of many
examples in the history of science of a change in our thinking that flowed
from the use of a new technique. Another such change is taking place
today as telecommunications and computing combine to produce new
ways of handling information. Cost apart, terrestrial distances are no
longer a barrier, for it is technically possible to use telecommunication
channels to distribute immense computing power backed by large stores
of data in such a way that its users are served as if they were in the same
room as the computer. If present trends continue, then by 1980 more
than 90 per cent of the world's computers would be linked to communication systems. This combination promises to be exceptionally important
because its effect will not be confined to one section of technology, nor
to technology alone. The collection and exchange of information under-
lies all that we do, and the structures and functions of industrial societies
depend absolutely on its prompt and ample supply. A major change in
information techniques is bound to affect every aspect of our lives—
economic, social, political, and domestic—and we need to be alert and
aware of what is happening if we aspire to direct its course.

The combination of computing and communications has not been
planned; the two constituents have followed quite independent evol-
utionary paths. Since its birth telecommunications has been a very
practical art, and only later did it acquire a theoretical base. It has from
the first been available for all to use in their daily lives and has required
no preliminary mental adjustment, for it was seen as a straightforward
extension of conversation and correspondence. Its seeming ordinariness
may be the reason why its revolutionary implications for the location
and organization of our affairs have taken so long to emerge. Business
men and politicians still huddle together within earshot of each other
and cling to rigid hierarchical patterns of organization despite the fact
that telecommunications' ability to girdle the earth seven times a second
challenged the need for either more than a century ago. For the most

part we have used telecommunications to do what we did before, but faster, instead of seeking to exploit its new potential.

The implications of computers have been obscured by their origin as the instruments of an esoteric mathematical cult, for it was not at first apparent that they had any practical relevance for commerce or affairs. Lady Lovelace[1] had indeed pointed out in the last century that it would be wrong to suppose that because Babbage's machine used the notation of arithmetic it was therefore restricted to that subject, but in this as in other matters connected with computing she was much too far ahead of her time and her warning was neither remembered nor understood. Many still think of computers as fast calculating machines and their manufacturers foster this misleading belief by advertising their wares in terms of millions of additions per second, as if it were important how many are done rather than for what purpose.

Convergence

These separate and superficially diverse techniques are now converging, first because each has begun to use the other. Computers are linked to distant users and to each other for the exchange of data and results; and telecommunications is moving cautiously but inevitably towards programmed control for the great flexibility of performance and wider range of facilities that if offers. As a subject for study, telecommunications has commonly been divided into three branches: terminal apparatus, signal transmission, and switching, but we now see that these pieces cover only one half of a wider scene. The three missing pieces are data storage, data processing, and programmed control, and these computing provides. No doubt the picture is still incomplete, but it represents a more natural selection out of the whole of life than does either constituent alone—and we have to stop somewhere. For the six-piece jigsaw the French have coined the term *l'informatique* but there is no corresponding English word, for the obvious transliteration has been appropriated as a trade name. For convenience of reference below the formula 'information engineering' is used, but it is not current.

As well as coming together in function, telecommunications and computing are converging in technology. This again is not the result of deliberate intent. What has happened is that the clamorous demands of computer designers have been forcing the growth of new techniques in electronics. Their demands have risen from two sources. First, the American defence and space programmes have had insatiable appetites for ever smaller, ever faster, ever more sturdy computers, and have also had the funds to ensure that they were forthcoming. Second, the rapidly expanding but nonetheless highly competitive commercial market for computers has been notable for the very hot pace of technical advance set by its dominant supplier—an understandable strategy for an oligopolist.

The overwhelming majority of computers are digital machines, and development effort has been concentrated on the handling of digital signals. The result has been dramatic, and current techniques for producing circuits by large-scale integration (LSI) now allow many hundreds of electronic components with all their interconnections to be manufactured very cheaply on a wafer of silicon only a few millimetres square; and these are early days. Telecommunciation engineers have recently rediscovered the merits of the digital signals with which they began, and they are fully seized of the advantages of riding on a band-wagon when the fare has been paid by others. As a consequence, computers and telecommunication equipment grow daily more alike and it cannot be long before both emerge from the same factory gate.

The separate paths followed by telecommunications and computing have led to the appearance of two separate groups of experts, each unfamiliar with the other's art, and this situation generates problems at two levels. At the technical level we have so far been able to rub along with a 'black box' approach relying on frontier controls (interface standards) to regulate the traffic between the computing and the communicating boxes. But this approach is exposed to all the risks of suboptimization, and as systems grow more extensive, more costly, and more complex it is becoming necessary for efficiency and security to design each system as a whole without prejudging questions of centralization or dispersal, separation or combination, of the communicating and computing functions and equipment. For this purpose we need a new group of experts covering the whole of information systems engineering.

An even more troublesome set of problems arises at the sociological level when we face the possible consequences for individuals and society of the development and widespread use of information systems. The elucidation and resolution of these problems are too important to be left to experts, and certainly not to two separate sets of experts who do not yet communicate effectively with each other; ordinary men and women must be closely involved. However, it is not easy for laymen to draw out the implications of an activity so embryonic, so well-defended by two layers of jargon, and so unnecessarily wrapped in mystique; the difficulties are compounded by the fact that neither group of experts is homogenous, for each has members drawn from the operators, the suppliers, the users, and the universities. Fig. 1 is highly schematic, but it presents a broad impression of the web of relationships.

We cannot afford to wait until information engineering has settled down, for if we were to do so we would drift into bad habits in default of wise policies; and we could then find ourselves facing some very unpleasant accomplished facts. Despite the difficulties, informed discussion is urgently needed, for the use of computers is no longer optional;

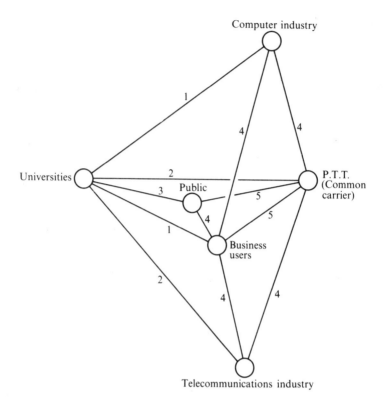

Fig. 1. The parties involved.
Nature of link:
(1) Computing science research and development
(2) Communications engineering research and development
(3) General education .
(4) Supply of goods and services
(5) Telecommunications services

they have become deeply embedded in the vitals of the management and control systems on which all industrial societies of the West rely—and the process is irreversible. Their coalescence with telecommunications is well advanced, and its completion will be pushed ahead by technological developments and pulled forward by market forces without reference to our wishes. There is here no cause for dismay, only for action. When we reflect how far the next decade may carry us it becomes clear that we must ensure that we progress towards goals of our own choosing if we are not be carried where we would prefer not to be.

This book does not pretend to identify all the problems, much less to solve them; its aim is to provide some background material against which a wider discussion can take place. The earlier chapters are some-what didactic and concentrate on telecommunications because books on computing abound. Moreover, computer men tend to dismiss telecommunications as a matter of a battery, a buzzer, and a length of wire.

Coding and signalling

Data and information

In the discussion of information engineering systems, 'data' means the spoken òr written words, letters, punctuation marks, numbers, or other symbols that are taken into the system for transmission, storage, or processing. These data commonly convey measurements or reports about some situation that concerns us, and we use the system to help us to assess their significance and to reassemble them in a convenient and comprehensive form. Information is an individual matter—what is news to me may not be news to you—but we need an objective measure of information when evaluating the performance of a system.

Following Shannon[2] in 1948, communication engineers have measured the information that a message conveys by the number of binary (yes—no) choices needed to select it from the entire set of alternative messages that can be transmitted. This measure expresses only the difficulty of transmitting the message; it says nothing about its news value or importance to its recipient. The binary choices made in selecting a message can be specified numerically by using the digits 0 and 1 to stand for *yes* and *no*, and the unit of information conveyed by a single choice is called a 'bit'—abbreviated from BInary digiT. Thus, two successive choices suffice to indicate from which cardinal point the wind is blowing, and so the amount of information conveyed is 2 bits. Increasing the precision to cover all 32 points marked on the mariner's compass would increase the amount of information to 5 bits, for $32 = 2^5$.

Shannon showed that we cannot increase the amount of information in data by processing them, but this does not mean that processing has no value, for the result may well take a more immediately useful form. Sometimes there may seem to be an increase in information, but this results from combining the input data with others previously entered and stored in the system. In practice, communication and computing unavoidably decrease the amount of information, for example by introducing errors, by limitations on precision, by incorrect analysis and by occasional losses caused by faulty equipment or operators' mistakes. It is a major objective in system design to keep this loss of information to acceptably low levels without incurring unacceptably high costs. One well-known method of combating errors is to repeat the transmission or the processing and to compare the results. Repetition is one way of introducing redundancy and complete repetition is not always necessary. An ordinary telegram, for instance, does not repeat the plain text but any figures are sent and printed twice; English spelling and syntax introduce their own redundancies and protect the text, but garbled numbers cannot be reconstructed. This topic is taken up in Chapter 3.

Analogue and digital data

Data can be represented in either analogue or digital form. Analogue representation uses the magnitude of some smoothly variable quantity to indicate the data, as a car's speedometer uses the continous displacement of a pointer over a scale to indicate the speed. Digital representation uses a separate stepping indicator for each of the digits which together express the numerical value of the data, as a car's odometer indicates the distance travelled. Microphones and television cameras convert the aural and visual data presented to them into electrical signals of the analogue type and their outputs have commonly been handled in this form. These signals can, however, be sampled at frequent intervals, the samples measured and the measurements expressed and transmitted as a stream of digital data. One such analogue-to-digital conversion known as pulse code modulation (PCM), is assuming increasing importance for ordinary telephone and television transmission as telecommunication systems are becoming adapted to carry digital signals. Analogue data are limited by precision of measurement, but with digital representation the precision can be increased by using more digits: for this reason, and because it makes less demand on the stability and accuracy of electronic circuits, it has become almost universal in data systems. The word 'data' unadorned can usually be taken to mean digital data unless the context or an explicit reference indicates the contrary.

Codes

When we exchange or record business data we do so most naturally in words and numbers using the familiar letters and arabic numerals of ordinary written or printed material in what is essentially a process of digitizing the analogue signals of speech. These characters were devised for human use and their recognition relies on our considerable skill in recognizing complex patterns irrespective of their scale, rotation, geometric distortion, colour, overlay, and so on. Even when they are ruthlessly and unpleasingly standardized in style, size, and position they are not convenient for automatic data communication or processing, for which purposes we use codes constructed from groups of highly simplified unit symbols. Typically, two unit symbols are employed (for example the dots and dashes of the Morse code) and such a code is called a binary code. The complete range of letters, figures, and other symbols covered by a code is called its 'alphabet' or 'character set'. The Morse code uses groups of different lengths, allocating the shorter groups to the most frequently used letters in order to minimize the time required to send a message in plain English. This technique, however, is applicable only when the frequency distribution of the characters in the messages to be transmitted is stable and known, and it does not apply to unrestricted numerical data.

For the completely automatic handling of data it is better to represent the characters in the alphabet by code groups of equal length. The problem then becomes one of choice, for we have to decide how many unit symbols each group should contain. Considerations of speed and efficiency suggest using a few units as possible, and the minimum number of units in the groups will depend on the number of characters required in the alphabet as well as on the number of different symbols employed. Thus, to represent only the ten decimal digits it suffices to use groups of:

(a) four binary symbols, for 2^4 is greater than 10, but 2^3 is not;
(b) three ternary symbols, for 3^3 is greater than 10, but 3^2 is not;
(c) two quarternary symbols, for 4^2 is greater than 10, but 4 is not;
(d) one decimal symbol, for $10 = 10$.

We have here a design trade-off between shorter code groups using a greater variety of unit symbols and the longest group, which uses binary symbols. The greater the variety the more likely is it that automatic equipment will confuse one symbol with another and introduce errors; binary coding offers security in this matter in exchange for the additional time required to handle its longer groups.

For commercial data we need an alphabet that includes at least the small and capital letters of the Roman alphabet, decimal digits, punctuation marks, and some other signs. A 7-unit binary code is widely used and provides for $2^7 = 128$ characters. One disadvantage of any universal code is that it is inefficient in special cases: thus for purely numerical data the 7-bit code wastes 7 bits on each decimal digit where 4 bits would do. Moreover, representing the data in decimal form rather than directly as binary numbers is inefficient, for an equivalent of about 3·3 bits per decimal digit suffices in pure binary notation—which gives more than twice the packing density of a 7-bit code. Conversion between the binary and decimal forms, however, adds to the cost and time of processing and a 4-bit 'binary coded decimal' is a common compromise.

Code standards

Telegraphy was the only common form of coded communication prior to the use of computers and a rather primitive 5-bit code ($2^5 = 32$)

has been standardized internationally by the CCITT (Comité Consultatif International Télégraphique et Téléphonique). The early development of computing took place in a context that was entirely independent of telegraphy, and it was also totally uncoordinated; each computer manufacturer developed his own codes and this at first caused little difficulty. However, the rapid growth of data-communication links between computers soon revealed a need for standards. Unfortunately the time never appears to be ripe for standardization; when it is attempted too early, before enough experience and understanding have been gained, standardization can cramp and stifle development. If it is attempted too late, the standards authority faces entrenched opposition from established users and suppliers who fear for their investments of time and money should their practice not be the chosen one. Because these interested parties necessarily provide the members of the standards committees the result can be an unedifying playing for time, a compromise that looks like one, or standardization *post mortem* in which agreement is reached only when the standard has become obsolescent and important interests no longer remain at risk. Sudden progress towards standardization is a common harbinger of a change of practice. Developments in electronics have made it practicable to provide substantial data-processing capacity in a single integrated circuit module. The use of these cheap single-chip processors to convert between different codes and formats may diminish the need to limit variety, and in this way offer great operational flexibility in future data-handling systems—as well as freeing some of our fellow men from the fatiguing pursuit of international standards.

There is a 7-bit American Standard Code for Information Interchange, more usually abbreviated to ASCII, and it has an international counterpart formulated by ISO (the International Standards Organization), which includes four characters for extending the alphabet. These 'escape characters' have similar functions to the shift keys on a typewriter; their use indicates that all subsequent characters are to be interpreted in terms of another alphabet. They are a most economical method of extension but have the significant disadvantage, as compared with using more code bits in each group, that when the escape character is missed or misread all subsequent characters will be misinterpreted; which phenomenon is well known to amateur typists.

Many computers handle data internally in groups of 8 bits which are known as 'bytes'. This has come about largely because of the development of magnetic tapes having 8 tracks for recording data signals with an additional, ninth, track for checking purposes, and also because one such byte can represent either two decimal digits (4 bits each) for closely packed numerical data, or one character of an 8-bit code ($2^8 = 256$) which is able to represent all the characters of the 7-bit ISO code plus those of the Cyrillic or other non-Roman alphabet, meteorological or

9

mathematical symbols, and so on. It is quite clear that we have not
reached the limit of expanding the alphabet. Thus, one scientific abstrac-
ting service requires an alphabet with about 700 characters to handle
the wide range of mathematical and technical symbols, and to cover
variations in typographic style and alignment, quite apart from point
size. It is safe to predict that 9-bit ($2^9 = 512$) codes will appear as computers begin to communicate with each other for the automatic control
of machine tools, manufacturing processes, and traffic of all kinds, and
as the cost and time penalties of handling longer code groups continue
to fall with the rapid advance of electronics. It is unlikely to be economic
to design one omni-purpose code to cover all of these specialist functions,
quite apart from others that will arise; and even within one specialism we
can expect to see effective standardization only where it grows naturally
out of a pressing need for widespread exchanges of data, and to the extent
that this need cannot economically be met by code conversion using
single-chip processors.

Signalling

So far we have been considering how data may be represented in coded
form, and have seen that a wide range of options exists. The methods
available for converting code groups into electrical signals for transmission
over wires or by radio waves present another wide range of alternatives.
There is first the broad choice between analogue and digital signals, but
because analogue signals are little used for data, and are slowly being
displaced for speech and television, we shall consider only digital signalling. Here again, because of its simplicity and robustness, there is a heavy
emphasis on binary signalling and it is convenient to focus the discussion
on it.

In essence, a telecommunication system comprises a sender, a receiver, and a medium that transmits electrical signals between them. In
radio systems the medium is a common one, and the longer telephone
and telegraph lines and cables also are shared by several users. Each user
is allocated his own separate 'channel' through the medium and the receiver is presented with some unwanted signals as well as the desired one.
Electrical noise and interference are also present and great ingenuity has
been applied to reducing the effects of these different disturbances. A
basic choice is whether to translate the units representing a character in,
say, a 7-bit code into seven successive binary signals for transmission one
after the other through a single channel, which is known as 'serial' working, or whether to transmit them 'in parallel' by sending the corresponding binary signals concurrently through seven separate channels. Broadly
speaking, serial working is cheaper but parallel working is faster, and the
choice often depends on the distance to be travelled. To transmit binary
signals a few metres from one room to another in the same building each

channel need consist only of a pair of wires, and the speed advantage of parallel working often outweighs the cost; intercontinental channels, however, are expensive and usually operate serially. In principle, parallel working could be extended beyond the seven bits of one character to the entire message, but this is most unlikely to prove economic even for very short distances because the extra speed that it would give is not worth the extra costs of the sender and receiver electronics associated with each channel. Nevertheless, pedants call the common form of parallel working 'serial by character, parallel by bit'.

The individual binary signals that represent the bits of the code are identical brief electrical impulses equal in duration and following each other at equal intervals of time, like the ticks of a clock. The '1' condition may be signalled by the presence of a pulse, and the '0' condition by the omission of a pulse from a regular sequence. In 'synchronous working' the receiver is equipped with an electronic clock that is maintained in synchronism with the sender's pulsing rate and it determines when the received signal shall be inspected to ascertain whether a pulse is present or not. Synchronization of sender and receiver can be achieved by transmitting occasional bursts of pulses from the sender's clock—for example, 16 pulses initially and repeated every few seconds. Alternatively, the data stream itself can be used, but it is then necessary to cover any long intervals between messages by generating and inserting 'idle' or 'padding' characters to fill the gaps and thus prevent a drift away from synchronism. This practice, elegantly called 'bit stuffing', is used also to prevent data signals from accidentally imitating the control signals used to initiate the setting up and the clearing down of the link. It may also be necessary to impose restraints on the sequence of digits, for instance that as a long-term average neither 1s nor 0s shall constitute less than 30 per cent of the digit stream, and that there shall never be more than, say, ten successive 0s. Synchronization presents difficult technical problems when international networks are linked, owing to the relatively long time of transmission over the network, and also to small fluctuations in this time when radio or satellite links are used. In these circumstances it may be necessary to use extremely stable clocks at each end of the channel and to align each with its national atomic standard of time. Inevitably in synchronous working the signalling speed is fixed and cannot be increased at will to take advantage of a particularly favourable conditions.

Alternatively 'asynchronous working' can be used: in this the message is divided into sections and each section is preceded by a distinctive 'start' signal which resets the receiver's clock. This clock has the same nominal rate as the one that controls the sender's pulsing rate so that the two are isochronous although not continously synchronized, and provided the message section is short enough the two clocks remain sufficiently in step not to cause errors. Often the section is only one character long, as in the start-stop code used by teleprinters, and this form of working is cheap and effective for low data rates. Clearly, asynchronous working requires extra signals that are different from the data signals and convey no part of the message; it is therefore less efficient in its use of the transmission channel. The longer the message section, the smaller is this loss of efficiency, but the greater is the risk of error caused by drift of the receiver's clock, and the larger is the amount of data lost should noise or interference initiate a false start.

We have also to decide how to signal the individual bits of each character. We can, for example, turn the current on and off, or we can reverse its flow, that is change its polarity. Again, when a succession of

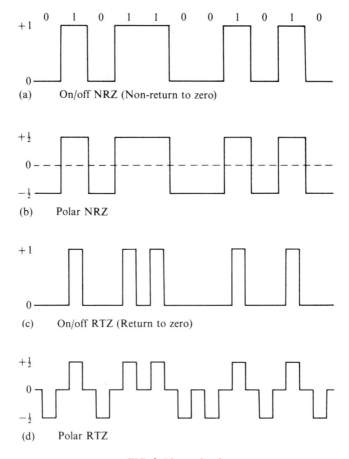

(a)   On/off NRZ (Non-return to zero)

(b)   Polar NRZ

(c)   On/off RTZ (Return to zero)

(d)   Polar RTZ

FIG. 2. Binary signals.

identical bits is to be signalled we can either return to the zero condition between each bit (RTZ), or we can simply maintain the same condition until the data changes (NRZ). Four possible combinations are illustrated in Fig. 2. One major difference is that on-off signalling involves a steady flow of current (that is, the transmission of a direct-current component) corresponding to the average height of the signal waveform above the baseline; polar signalling does not. Public telecommunication systems, having been developed for the telephone, do not, apart from the direct connections to the local exchange, provide for the transmission of direct current signals. Again, of the two methods of polar signalling (Fig. 2(b) and 2(d)) the non-return-to-zero method involves longer periods of

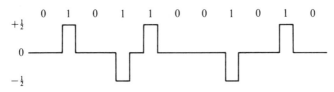

(a) Bipolar (no signal for 0, ± alternately for 1)

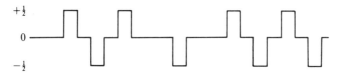

(b) Polar differential (signals only for changes 0 to 1, or vice versa)

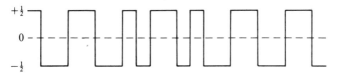

(c) Phase modulation (signals + to − for 0, − to + for 1)

FIG. 3. Binary signals.

current on and fewer changes in polarity, and this implies a higher average signal power. This disadvantage is avoided by the 'Bi-polar' method of signalling shown in Fig. 3(a), and also by the 'differential' or 'change-of-state' method of Fig. 3(b). Another method used is 'phase modulation', which is shown in Fig. 3(c).

It will be evident that a variety of choice faces the would-be communicator: in practice, the choice is wider still for Figs. 2 and 3 do not exhaust the possibilities, moreover (as we shall consider below) the basic signals have to be packaged to suit the characteristics of the particular type of communication channel being used. When to these options we add the choice between synchronous and asynchronous working, and the choices of alphabet and of code, it is clear that we have a complicated situation. It would be very nice if it were possible to standardize on one alphabet, one code, and one method of signalling, but users' requirements differ and no one standard is the best in all circumstances. Nor are the codes and methods used for transmitting data the same as those used for processing it inside computers. Additional data-code conversion processes are therefore necessary at input and output, and these incur penalties in cost, time, and error. The trend is strongly towards a much closer integration of communication and computing, and in the long term we can hope to see a reduction of the number of variants in use. On the other hand the trend towards code conversion using ever-cheaper single-chip processors could make standardization an irrelevant issue. It remains to be seen where the balance of commercial and economic advantage will lie. In the meantime there is no one best choice, and no substitute for expert advice.

3

Bandwidth, distortion, and error

Bandwidth

] The transmission of electrical signals is subject to influences that resemble those of elasticity, inertia, and resonance in mechanical systems; thus, in the middle of the nineteenth century the pioneers of submarine telegraphy found that there was a practical limit to the number of times per second that turning the current on and off could be detected at the distant end. | When they attempted to go faster the electrical resistance and capacitance of the cable absorbed and blurred their signals. Earlier in the same century Fourier had shown that for the purpose of analysis a periodic oscillation of any form could be replaced by a mixture of sinusoidal oscillations consisting of a fundamental plus a series of harmonics. It is, for example, the number and strengths of the harmonics which determine the quality of a musical sound, and which are characteristic of different instruments sounding the same note. Again, the 100 bits/second polar RTZ signal that corresponds to the recurring, if rather uninformative, data sequence 0, 1, 0, 1, 0, 1 . . . repeats itself at intervals of 1/50 second, and thus comprises a fundamental oscillation with a frequency of 50 Hz† and its harmonics. Fourier analysis shows that when—as here— the second half of a wave is an upside-down copy of its first half then only the odd harmonics are present, in this case $(3 \times 50) = 150$ Hz, $(5 \times 50) = 250$ Hz, 350 Hz, 450 Hz and so on. Clearly, the faster the rate of signalling the higher will be the frequencies of the fundamental and its harmonics. A signal with the idealized rectangular waveform of Fig. 2 (Ch. 2) has a harmonic series that extends to infinity, with harmonic components whose amplitudes decrease as their frequencies increase. More complex signals comprise several fundamental oscillations with their separate harmonic series.

⌊ Signal transmission involves the transfer of energy, each of the harmonics carries some part of the total energy of the signal, and the distribution of this energy in terms of frequency is referred to as the

† 1 hertz (Hz) equals one complete vibration per second; also 1 kHz = 1000 Hz, 1 MHz = 1000 kHz, 1 GHz = 1000 MHz.

Signals

15

'spectrum' of the signal. The analogy is with optical spectra, in which the concentration or dispersion of energy determines the colour seen. The spectrum of the 100 bits/second signal already mentioned is illustrated in Fig. 4(a) which shows that only the odd harmonics are present, and that their relative amplitudes diminish as their frequencies increase.

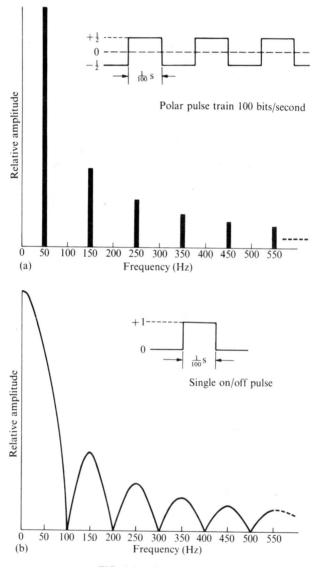

FIG. 4. Baseband spectra.

The amount of energy conveyed by each harmonic component is proportional to the square of its amplitude, and so their relative shares of the total signal energy decrease much more rapidly than the figure suggests. The spectrum shown in Fig. 4(b) is for an isolated on-off pulse having the same duration (1/100 second) as the individual pulses of the 100 bit/second signal of Fig. 4(a). The figures differ in two respects. First, because the signal of Fig. 4(b) is on-off rather than polar it has a direct-current component—shown at zero frequency. Second, because it is not repetitive it has no fundamental frequency and no harmonics and its spectrum exhibits a 'continuous' rather than a 'line' distribution of energy. The frequency range covered by the spectrum of a signal is known as its 'baseband', and the extent of the baseband (in Hz) is the signal's 'bandwidth'. Bandwidth is one of the basic concepts in telecommunications, for it is used also in specifying the signalling capability of a cable or radio link—the greater the bandwidth, the wider the frequency range that can be transmitted, and so the higher the maximum rate of signalling that is possible.

In practice, it is usually expensive to increase the bandwidth of a link and advantage is taken of the fact that it is not necessary to transmit the entire spectrum of a signal. For example, although the spectrum of an ideal rectangular signal extends to infinity its higher reaches contain only a tiny fraction of the signal's energy, cutting them off merely rounds the corners and inclines the verticals in the waveform and when done judiciously it causes no practical difficulty (See also Appendix §1). Thus, although the baseband of the 100 bits/second polar RTZ signal of our example ranges from 50 Hz to infinity it can be quite adequately transmitted through a link with a bandwidth of no more than 100 Hz.

This example, and that of the submarine cable, indicate that it is necessary to relate the spectrum of the signal to the characteristics of the channel used to convey it. In 1928 Nyquist expressed one aspect of this relationship in his 'Sampling Theorem' which states that a signal with a spectrum limited to the frequency range 0 to W Hz, and lasting T seconds, can be completely specified by $2TW$ numbers.[3] The theorem implies that a channel can transmit a repetitive 0, 1, 0, 1, 0, 1 . . . binary data signal at the rate of 2 bits/second for each 1 Hz of its bandwidth. In telegraphy the unit of signalling is called the 'Baud', after Baudot, an early pioneer. For binary signals this unit is equivalent to 1 bit/second, which has led to the two terms being used loosely as synonyms; but they are not so for a multi-level signal (see Appendix, §2).

The technical constraints on bandwidth are least when radio waves are propagated through free space, but because space is free for all to use there is keen competition for radio channels and care has to be taken to conserve this scarce and unique natural resource. We have a public duty to employ radio transmission sparingly and appropriately and, when

17

we *can* justify using it, to employ signals of the lowest possible power, in the narrowest bandwidth, and curbed in geographical spread by the use of highly directional aerials. The opposite extreme is that costly capital investment a submarine cable equipped with amplifiers; in it, the signal bandwidth that can be transmitted depends upon the materials and dimensions of the cable, and on the spacing of the submerged amplifiers. The closer the amplifiers the broader the band, but the greater the cost and the higher the risk of failure. Hence, the available bandwidth is subject to severe economic constraints, and there is great emphasis on parsimony in its use. The bandwidth required depends on the signalling method; thus, the bit sequence and rate of our earlier example corresponded to a fundamental frequency of 50 Hz when sent as a polar RTZ signal, but the use of a bipolar signal would reduce the fundamental frequency to 25 Hz and thus halve the required bandwidth. There would, however, be an increase in the cost and complexity of the sending and receiving equipments, and a balance has to be struck for each particular case.

For short local links it is possible to transmit signals at very high rates over an ordinary twisted pair of wires; one such system uses amplifiers at intervals of 300 metres and works at 500 000 bits/second. Longer links commonly make use of national telephone systems, and for general use these offer channels of three kinds:

(*a*) narrow-band telegraph channels provided by sub-dividing telephone channels, and used at rates of 50 to 200 bits/second;

(*b*) speech-band channels used at 500 to 5000 bits/second;

(*c*) broadband channels provided to carry groups of 12 speech channels, and used for data at rates of 40 000 bits/second.

In considering these rates it is worth recalling that untrained users operate keyboards at about 1 character per second, that is at less than 10 bits/second, and do so somewhat sporadically. In order to make a more efficient use of a data channel the signals generated by such a user may be accumulated in a local buffer store and discharged in bursts to the channel at its normal working rate; between bursts the channel would be released, or signals from other operators would be inserted. Channels such as (*b*) or (*c*) can carry a single high-speed signal, but it is often more useful to divide their use between several slow-speed signals by a process known as multiplexing. Two methods are commonly used: frequency-division multiplex (FDM), and time-division multiplex (TDM).[3]

TDM is the simpler in concept, for it merely consists in interleaving several independent data signals by allowing each the sole use of the broadband channel for regular, repeated, brief periods. Consider, for instance four data signals A, B, C, D each having a rate of 25 bits/second and together sharing a channel capable of 100 bits/second. 'A' would be connected to the channel for a period of 1/100 second and send a quarter-length sample of its current signal, B would have the next similar period, then C, D, A, B, C . . . Within the common channel the signals would be indistinguishable from a single 100 bits/second signal, for only at its distant end are they distributed in rotation to the four quarter-speed outlets. Time division was invented in 1874 when Baudot combined six 15 bits/second telegraph channels onto one line, but with the rise of telephony it was eclipsed by frequency division for this was more obviously suited to the analogue signals of speech. The development of computers and of data transmission has restored TDM to favour because it is well adapted to digital signals, and because integrated circuit electronics more easily handles digital than analogue signals. Indeed, the trend away from TDM has now reversed as telephone and television signals are being handled in digital form.

FDM displaces the data signal's spectrum from its baseband position by 'modulating' the data signal onto a higher frequency 'carrier wave'. The result is re-distribute the signal's energy on either side of the carrier frequency, and by using a series of carrier frequencies spaced to accommodate the spectra of adjacent signals without overlapping it is possible to fill the available bandwidth with a number of independent low-speed signals travelling through the broadband channel in parallel. The principle is essentially the same as the familiar sharing of the broadcast band by a number of independent radio stations working on different wavelengths, that is, on different carrier frequencies. As in broadcasting, either amplitude or frequency modulation can be used (see Appendix, §§ 3 to 6), and the device used to impress the data signals onto the carrier wave and to recover them at the distant end is called a modulator-demodulator, or more concisely a 'modem'. Another use of modems is to locate the spectrum of a single data signal in the optimum part of a speech-band channel, for example to keep it clear of the edges of the band and also to avoid clashes with the housekeeping signals used in the telephone system itself to control the setting-up, clearing-down, and metering of calls.

Modems

Modulation is simple in principle, but the need to match the performance of the sending and receiving equipment leads to practical difficulties when modems supplied by different manufacturers are installed at the two ends of a link, as when independent users are able to buy their own modems and to dial a connection to any other user over the public network. Compatibility can be assured by setting a sufficiently tight specification for modem performance, but when imposed by the telephone authorities this approach invites criticism on the grounds of restrictiveness and increased cost. In general, the telephone authorities would prefer to provide and maintain the modems used with their networks. In part, this is because they have long been accustomed to provide their customers with an overall service—from mouth to ear—without having to guarantee the use or the detailed technical performance of specific routes or equipment; and they see the modem as a convenient buffer which will preserve their freedom to develop and rearrange their networks as their technical, economic, and operational needs require. They are concerned also at the troubles which split responsibility for the supply and maintenance of the total link (modems plus cable) can bring to both themselves and to their data customer—troubles which could be aggravated by cut-price competition in the sale of modems. The data users, on the other hand, fear that the authorities will adopt a safety first, Rolls-Royce, approach to modem design, and be too conservative in their attitudes to investment and obsolescence, and in these ways deny them the benefits of reduced costs and increased performance which the rapid pace of development in electronics is making possible. It seems clear, at least, that there is little chance of striking the best economic balance unless the design of modems and of links is considered as a whole, for otherwise each set of designers will tend to pare down his own costs by throwing a larger share of the total burden onto the other side. Who should provide, and who maintain, data modems has been the subject of hot debate—and seems likely to remain so. The problems raised are further complicated by the hectic growth of data traffic between different national systems, with all the implications that this has for international standardization.

Distortion

It is not possible to transmit electrical signals through a telecommunications channel without change. In a radio system virtually the whole of the energy emitted by the transmitting aerial is dissipated as heat, in a short-wave channel, for example, the energy received and used may be much less than one million millionth of the sender's output. Telephone cables also attenuate the signals they transmit, and typically their attenuation increases as the signalling frequency increases. Thus, a telephone channel may reduce the power of a signal four times as much at 100 Hz and at 3000 Hz as it does at 1000 Hz; nor are telephone channels designed to transmit direct currents. Attenuation of the signal has two unpleasant effects. First, by altering the shape of the signal's spectrum it changes its waveform (see Appendix, § 1). Second, the signal gradually sinks into the general background of electrical noise and interference which is always present.

The distortion can be tackled by passing the signal through 'attenuation equalizers', which are electrical networks designed to have a transmission characteristic that is the inverse of the channel's; their correction can never be exact, and economic design aims only at achieving an acceptable result. The general loss of signal energy can be dealt with by using electronic amplifiers to boost the signal, such amplifiers are called 'repeaters' by telecommunication engineers. Channels with bandwidths of several million Hertz can be provided over cables by amplifying the signals every few kilometres when their energy has fallen to rather less than 1/100 000 of its initial value, and before they have sunk too deeply into the accompanying noise. However, what noise is present is amplified along with the signal, and there is an inescapable accumulation of noise in long links. Digital signals can be 'regenerated' to offset the cumulative effects of distortion and noise, in effect, a long link is divided into a number of short sections and the signal received from one section is used to initiate the generation of a properly shaped and correctly timed new signal for onward transmission over the next section. Regeneration allows the deterioration of the signal to be arrested and, provided the sections can be kept sufficiently short, removes any practical limit on the terrestrial distances that can be worked.

The speed of transmission of electrical signals is very high, for it approaches the speed of light; at this speed radio signals can round the world in one-seventh of a second, and signals travel over broadband cables at speeds of the same order. For most purposes the resulting time delays are not troublesome, but they can become so when using artificial satellites for these introduce an extra delay as a consequence of their very high orbits—36 000 km above the earth. The ¼-second delay that arises with each hop to and from a satellite is not too disturbing for telephony, but it may upset the operation of some automatic checking and control systems. Again, although these satellites are nominally stationary relative to the earth's surface they do wander slightly in position, and their movement causes small variations in delay that add to the problems of synchronization.

As well as delaying all signals most telecommunication channels are dispersive and delay signals or signal components lying in certain frequency ranges more than those in others. For example, an ordinary telephone channel can delay signal components near the edge of its band by 2 or 3 milliseconds relative to those nearer the centre. This has no significant effect on speech, but it is large compared with the 0·2 millisecond that separates adjacent data bits when signalling at 5000 bits/second. The result is a 'delay' or 'phase' distortion that can be corrected by equalization networks having the appropriate inverse characteristics. As for attenuation equalizers, the correction cannot be exact, and an economic balance has to be struct at some acceptable level of distortion. To specify this level is no easy task, but it is quite practicable to reduce the distortion to one-tenth of its uncorrected value.

An important source of both attenuation and of phase distortion is the generation of echoes of the primary signal which arrive after brief delays and combine with it. Echoes are a universal plague: they arise in short-wave radio systems by multiple reflections from the ionosphere;

they arise in microwave systems by similar reflections from stratified layers in the atmosphere and from large obstacles; they arise in cable systems by reflections from the residual physical irregularities introduced where cable lengths are jointed together, and where cables are connected to sending, receiving or amplifying equipment. When the link is long enough for the main echoes to be delayed by 45 milliseconds or more they can be disturbing to telephone users, and telephone channels of this length are fitted with 'echo suppressors' which operate by interrupting the return path. However, echoes which are strong enough to disturb a telephone conversation are too feeble to upset data transmission, and when a long-distance telephone channel is used for data it is usual to send an initial burst of a few second of 2100 Hz tone in order to disable the echo suppressors, and thus permit data transmission simultaneously in both directions. Although echoes are a great nuisance, artificial echoes can be generated and used as a means of correcting both attenuation and phase distortion (see Appendix, § 7).

Noise

All communication channels are infested with the unwanted and meaningless signals which are usually called noise because in audio circuits they produce an unwelcome hissing and crackling. In television channels 'noise' produces dark and bright spots on the picture, and in bad cases a veritable snowstorm; in data channels 'noise' produces errors in the interpretation of the received signals. Some noise comes from imperfections in the equipment—faulty contacts, switching transients, vibration of defective joints and so on; this noise takes the form of brief impulses (crackles). Switching noise is most troublesome in channels routed through city centres, and is most intense in the traditional busy hours of the working day. Other sources of noise are inherent in the atomic nature of matter and electricity, and noise of this origin has a random waveform (hiss). Radio channels are disturbed by noise of both kinds generated by natural electrical phenomena in the atmosphere and outside it. In general, data transmission is less vulnerable to random noise than it is to impulse noise, for the latter may resemble a spurious data bit. The result is to introduce errors when the ratio of signal amplitude to noise amplitude is too small. The spectra of noise signals tends towards a roughly even distribution of energy across the band, hence the signal-to-noise ratio can be improved by reducing the bandwidth accepted by the receiver to the minimum required by the data signal. Again, because the received noise is independent of the signal's amplitude it makes sense to send at the maximum possible power. There is a well-known theoretical relation between signalling power and noise power for effective operation (see Appendix § 8), but there are unfortunately equally well-established practical reasons why working systems fall far short of the ideal.

Another kind of unwanted signal is picked up from adjacent channels; known from its telephony context as 'crosstalk' it is less troublesome in data links. Crosstalk may be caused by residual electromagnetic couplings between channels when there is insufficient screening or imperfect electrical balance between adjacent pairs of wires in the same cable. It can arise from insufficient limitation of bandwidth at the sender or the receiver—a situation familiar to anyone who has used a cheap set to listen to medium-wave broadcasting, and it can arise from the use of equipment that has a non-linear response. Thus, the repeaters in a broadband cable system have to amplify many independent signals presented to them simultaneously, and when faulty or overloaded, or if they have been inadequately designed, the relation between input signal amplitude and output signal amplitude ceases to be a linear one and then the signals modulate each other causing 'intermodulation crosstalk'. Cables of this kind are very widely used in telephone systems, and the design of their repeaters exploits the sporadic character of speech. No multichannel telephone system is designed to carry all of its channels operating simultaneously at full power, for this never occurs and it would be quite uneconomic to provide for it. However, difficulties can arise when too many data signals are presented to the system, for these tend to remain at full power all the time.

Non-linearity can also be caused by imperfect switch contacts, and by the magnetic overloading of ferrous materials. Again, some telephone channels are designed to compress the amplitude range of the input speech at the sending end, and to expand it again after reception. This process is known as 'companding' and in an noisy long-distance channel it improves the signal-to-noise ratio of the received speech by keeping the signalling level high without risk of overloading; but, because the compression and expansion cannot be instantaneous nor precisely complementary some non-linearity occurs, and this can cause trouble when the channel is used for data, especially when amplitude modulation is employed.

Frequency-division multiplex systems commonly employ single-sideband suppressed carrier transmission in order to economise in the use of bandwidth, and signal distortion occurs when the locally generated carrier which is re-introduced at the receiving end is incorrect in frequency. However, the CCITT standard specifies a maximum error of ±2 Hz which causes difficulty for data transmission only when narrow-band frequency modulation is used.

Various methods have been devised for offsetting deficiencies in transmission. Amplification, regeneration, and equalization have already been mentioned. Equalization is usually accomplished at the receiving end, but it is possible to give a signal a compensating distortion before transmission—a process sometimes called pre-emphasis. This has an obvious economic advantage when a central point is sending to a large number of distant receivers over channels having similar characteristics, as in broadcasting; it can however give the transmitted signal a more 'peaky' waveform and thus lead to non-linear distortion by overloading amplifiers. Fixed equalizers can be designed and fitted to leased private channels, but when data are transmitted through the ordinary public switched network the channels that happen to be picked up by the switches in the telephone exchanges will change from call to call and an adaptable equalizer is necessary. This is most readily provided by the echo technique, and by using standard test signals to precede the data message it is possible to arrange for automatic self-equalization.

In leased channels impulse noise can be reduced by choosing routes that avoid the busier exchanges, and by empirical selection among alternative channels over a given route. This type of noise is most disturbing when the impulse maintains the form of a sharp peak, and this occurs only when all its spectral components maintain their correct relative timings. By passing the received signal, with its accompanying noise, through an 'all-pass' network which alters the phases of these components without affecting their relative amplitudes the impulse noise peaks can be spread out in time and reduced in height by as much as ten times. The signal pulses are of course similarly affected by the network but they are protected by using a complementary network at the sending end, and because this technique spreads the signal out before transmission and gathers it together again afterwards it is known as 'Smear-desmear'. Radio transmission is particularly prone to disturbance and uses automatic gain control (to offset fading) and automatic frequency control (to offset receiver tuning drift). Short-wave channels employing ionospheric reflection suffer from variable echo distortions caused by simultaneous transmission over alternative paths, and echoes with delays of up to 5 millisecond can occur. Highly-directive aerials are used to select signals from one path only, and in diversity reception several such aerials are used with the receiving channel connected automatically to whichever of them is producing the strongest signal. Multipath and multimode propagation also occur when electromagnetic waves are transmitted through copper pipes or dielectric rods used as waveguides, and a variety of means has been devised to suppress unwanted modes of transmission.

It is not possible to correct or compensate for every source of signal distortion, and some residual disturbances remain in all practical links. Their effects are different for different methods of transmission. Where distances are short, the baseband transmission of polar signals is simple, economical and effective. Amplitude modulation, also, is simple and effective when the amplitude of the received signal is stable and there is not too much noise, and it is very little affected by carrier frequency offset. Double-sideband suppressed-carrier AM with synchronous detection is very effective against noise but requires more complicated equipment, and both it and simple AM require twice the bandwidth of baseband transmission for a given data rate. Vestigial- and single-sideband working require less bandwidth but more complex sending and receiving equipment. Frequency modulation is simple, it permits either synchronous or asynchronous signalling and works acceptably over a wide range of channel conditions; and it is the most widely used method of data transmission. Phase modulation is particularly effective against noise, but relatively complex in equipment. The very wide variety of alternatives has to be assessed in terms of the particular circumstances of each case, taking account of the distances, the characteristics of the available channels and of any other services which share their use, the operating speeds, and of course the user's evaluation of his own needs and acceptable costs. The assessment will change as electronic equipment continues to develop and to fall in cost, and will move in favour of more complex systems.

Errors and error protection

When everything that is economically acceptable has been done to protect and recover the signal from distortion and noise, the number of residual errors—that is, incorrectly interpreted bits—is typically in the range 3 to 30 per million, although it can be as high as 1000 per million for short-wave radio. For a given method of transmission the error rate will be higher for longer links, and it depends on the signalling speed; thus, in a typical channel set up through the automatic telephone system the bit error rate might range from 2 per million when signalling at 600 bits/second to 5 at 1200 bits/second and 12 at 2400 bits/second. It is, therefore usual to protect the data message against corruption by these residual errors by using coding techniques that employ the principle of redundancy to detect errors. Ideally, the optimum balance would be struck between signal protection and code protection in each case, but the pressures of practical life usually force a more ready-made approach. Because code protection requires the transmission of checking bits or characters additional to the 'naked code' which conveys the data, it reduces the effective capacity of the channel, and it requires extra equipment for coding and checking. However, equipment costs are falling and the economic balance is tipping towards more complex code protection (see Appendix §9).

It is feasible in data transmission systems to reduce the residue of undetected errors to any desired level at relatively little cost, and protection is certainly needed to a higher degree than telecommunicators have been used to provide for telegraphy, for telegraph messages are subject to human checks which deploy resources of spelling, grammar, and context that are less readily available in automatic systems. However, there is a law of diminishing returns in error control, and it is important to recollect that the number of errors introduced by human operators engaged in data capture and entry can be much greater than the number introduced by even uncorrected data links. Coding methods can be used to reduce the residual error rate from 10 per million bits to 1 per 100 millions, or even lower, but 1 error per 100 million bits corresponds to less than one letter wrong in a complete copy of The Bible—although at the 120 megabits/second of a very wideband channel it also corresponds to more than an error a second.

It is important to examine carefully the consequences of residual errors for these will vary with the application. When the data are being used to keep a file up to date, say a bank account, the effects of errors will be cumulative and persistent. But in a telemetry system a rare out-of-line reading can be treated as a temporary aberration and ignored—as is the custom in scientific work! There will usually be a practical, economic, limit beyond which it is not sensible to go in the reduction of transmission errors. When a computer designer is asked what error rate he can tolerate in his data transmission links, he first thinks in terms of none; but to take him literally would involve infinite cost and infinite time to check its achievement, and he can usually be persuaded to consider the economic and operational circumstances of his actual system.

Much misplaced ingenuity has been wasted on the theoretical design of protected codes to meet circumstances simplified to suit the mathematics, such as purely random noise, or to cope with the particular pattern of noise observed during a specific series of tests. However convenient this may be we need to remember always that a telecommunication system is not a static entity; its plant grows, decays, and is renewed, and the channels provided through it are rearranged to cope with new demands, to by-pass faults, to bring new broadband links into use, or to allow obsolete equipment to be withdrawn from service. Traffic patterns change seasonally, during the day, and during the working week; they are affected by public events, they change slowly with the growth of the system, with shifts in population, and to meet changing business and social circumstances. Channels set up through the switched network follow different routes depending on the fluctuating incidence of other calls competing for the use of the same equipment. The error rate and its pattern change for all of these reasons, and it can soar to stratospheric heights when engineers are working to repair, test, instal, or rearrange channels. There is no substitute for measurements on the actual channels which are to be used, but even for them the results have to be treated as a statistical sample—indicative, but not definitive. None of this provides any ground for legitimate criticism of the telephone authorities; in the past they have contracted to supply an adequate and economic service for human conversation; they have not guaranteed to do this by any particular technical means, or over specified routes, nor to maintain specific technical standards. It would be a surprising coincidence if economic design for telephony had produced a system equally suitable for data transmission, for this poses novel and more exacting requirements; and it also faces the authorities with a new and unusually well-informed, if occasionally unreasonable, set of customers.

4

By land and sea, through air and space

Physical connections

The simplest communication link is the pair of thin insulated copper
wires that joins a telephone—or a data terminal—to its local exchange.
This kind of link is often called a 'physical pair' in order to distinguish
it from a channel formed by multiplexing over a broadband link. The
pair is usually laid up with several hundred others inside a lead sheath
and no more economic alternative has yet been devised for local-end
connections. However, future services such as cable television may well
require wideband links for local distribution and these would be very
suitable for high-speed data transmission also. The existing local distribution networks of national telephone systems form a large part of
their heavy investment; as such, they are much more likely to be ex-
ploited than abandoned, as some have suggested. Cheap electronic
modules drawing their power from the telephone line may be used to
provide digital services over these networks at much higher data rates
than the few thousands of bits per second now achieved. The future
will be determined by long-term economic trends which it is impossible
to predict with assurance; thus, should the price of metals continue to
rise and that of electronics continue to fall then it could become worth
working the local networks as copper and lead mines, replacing the
existing cables with small coaxial tubes having aluminium conductors,
or with microwave radio links. Its very simplicity has meant that the
local network has been a poor relation at the technological feast, for
the greater glamour of long-distance wideband links has fascinated the
better brains; but as a result the cost balance has shifted and we can
expect to see substantial movement in what has been something of a
stagnant backwater.

Bearer systems

When a narrow-band data signal has reached its local telephone exchange over a cable pair, it is passed forward over a similar, but somewhat
thicker, pair in one of the junction cables that link adjacent exchanges.

In this manner, if the signal has a remote destination, it passes to the
terminal equipment of the long-distance network. Various techniques are
in use for long-distance transmission; they provide wideband bearer channels
which are divided by multiplexing into narrower channels, typically of the
4 kHz bandwidth needed for carrying speech signals in the range 300 to
3400 Hz. Frequency-division multiplexing is the most common method
and uses successive stages of single-sideband suppressed-carrier amplitude-
modulation to build up the wide-band signal, for example in Britain:

1 speech channel	0–4 kHz
12 speech channels = 1 group	60–108 kHz
5 groups (60 channels) = 1 basic super-group	312–552 kHz
15 super-groups (900 channels) = 1 basic hyper-group	312–4028 kHz
3 hyper-groups (2700 channels)	312–12 336 kHz
or 12 hyper-groups (10 800 channels)	4404–59 580 kHz

Time-division multiplexing systems are, however, rapidly coming into
service for telephony, and are particularly well-suited to data. No standard has yet been established, but the pattern might be:

96 data channels × 600 bits/second	
or 24 data channels × 2400 bits/second	64 kbits/second
or 6 data channels × 9600 bits/second	
32 channels × 64 kbits/second	2·048 Mbits/second
4 channels × 2·048 Mbits/second	8·5 Mbits/second
14 channels × 8·5 Mbits/second	120 Mbits/second
4 channels × 120 Mbits/second	500 Mbits/second

This last data rate of 500 Mbits/second corresponds to transmitting the
whole of The Bible in less than one-tenth of a second.

Coaxial cables

Probably the most common bearer system employs coaxial pairs
(tubes) which consist of a copper conductor mounted centrally on
polythene spacers along the axis of a cylindrical copper sheath. In
Britain, two sizes of tubes are in service, of 4·4 mm and 9·5 mm outside
diameters. The signal attenuation of a coaxial pair increases as the frequency rises and decreases with increased diameter. Hence, the wider
the bandwidth required the more frequently is it necessary to insert
amplifiers (repeaters) to boost the failing signals. For a 9·5 mm coaxial
tube an upper frequency limit of 12 MHz is possible with repeaters at
intervals of 4 km, and reducing the repeater spacing to 1·5 km enables
signals up to 60 MHz to be used. A large coaxial cable may contain as
many as 18 separate tubes, 9 for each direction of transmission, and
thus be able to bear almost 100 000 both-way telephone channels. When

used for time-division-multiplex systems, or for data, a 4·4-mm tube
can carry signals at the rate of 120 Mbits/second, and should be capable
of development to 400 Mbits/second, with perhaps twice this rate for a
9·5-mm tube.

Coaxial tubes of larger diameter, 38 mm, are used in submarine cables.
A transatlantic tube of this type may have repeaters at intervals of about
10 km and bear almost 2000 telephone channels in each direction in the
band 0·3 to 14 MHz. The use of such cables over inter-continental distances inevitably introduces appreciable transmission delays; thus, the
U.K. to Australia channel is 31 000 km long, and its signal transmission
time is 130 milliseconds, which corresponds to transmission at rather
more than three-quarters of the speed of light. Increasing the bandwidth
means reducing the repeater spacing and so increasing the number of
submerged repeaters for a given route, and this imposes much heavier
penalties for a submarine cable than for a land route. The development
of more compact and more reliable electronics has changed the economics
of submarine cable operation very considerably: the first transatlantic
telephone cable carried only 36 channels, but 20 years later a cable was
laid at three times the cost to provide 50 times as many channels. Practical limitations are set by the problems of feeding power to operate the
repeaters, which has to be done from the two shore ends, and by the
great cost of recovering and replacing a faulty repeater, but there seems
to be no technical reason why development to 10 000 or even 30 000
telephone channels should not be achieved, and be economic for the
more heavily loaded routes.

Microwave radio

The next most popular way of providing long-distance communication
is by microwave radio, using frequency-modulated carrier waves in frequency ranges near 2, 4, 6, and 11 GHz to provide wideband bearer
channels. Radio transmission at these frequencies is basically line-of-sight,
for the wavelengths (3 to 15 cm) are too short to allow effective propagation by diffraction around such major obstacles as hills or large build-
ings. The use of height plus highly directional aerials assists the rejection
of unwanted signals reflected from the ground, which otherwise cause
echo distortion; echoes can also occur under some weather conditions
by reflection from stratified layers in the atmosphere. A typical microwave system links two major cities 200 km apart by a chain of intermediate relay stations located on hilltops 30 to 60 km apart, and provides
eight independent radio channels sharing the same stations and aerials.
Seven of these are working bearer channels and the eighth acts as a common standby; each channel is able to carry 2 Hypergroups (1800 both-
way telephone channels) or an equivalent 120 Mbits/second of data. In
a country as small as Britain there is great competition for the use of the

few available hills suitable for hops of up to 60 km along the main inter-
city routes, and because these tend to be in areas of some scenic beauty
the erection of aerials is opposed on amenity grounds, for microwave
masts and towers have not yet acquired the nostalgic charm of those
products of an earlier technology–the windmills. Congestion of the few
available routes produces heavy pressure on the available frequencies
and there is a continual drive to exploit higher frequencies. The 11 GHz
band is expected to be suitable for digital signals at rates up to 120
Mbits/second over 30 km paths. The 15 GHz band, also, is promising;
although at this frequency large raindrops can absorb and scatter the
signals. However, because adequate ground clearance is more easily
achieved at these shorter wavelengths echo distortion is reduced, propagation is non-dispersive, and 15 GHz signals should be suitable for data
rates as high as 500 Mbits/second over paths of 5 to 10 km. The risk of
disturbance by rain remains, but because heavy rain is often very local
it may be practicable to provide a network of alternative paths and use
automatic re-routing to skirt round the showers. Even higher frequencies
up to 100 GHz (3 mm wavelength) may prove useful over distances of a
kilometre or so, say for local distribution. The very wide spectrum
available, and their high data capacity could make these frequencies
valuable for intra-base links, for example for linking shops to their local
banks.

Communication satellites

More than half the world's international channels are provided by
microwaves on carrier frequencies of 4 to 6 GHz by using artificial
satellites as the intermediate relay stations of two-hop microwave links.
The first communication satellites were injected into low orbits, and
remained within range of one earth station for only an hour or two.
Today, the favoured technique uses the equatorial orbit that has a rotation period of 24 hours, which means that the satellite remains stationary
relative to the earth's surface, and therefore is continually within range.
One such satellite can 'see' and serve about one-third of the earth's
surface. A disadvantage of this geostationary orbit is its height, 36 000 km
above ground level, for this introduces a transmission delay of about
0·25 second. A single satellite link is not too troublesome for speech, but
as more than one is needed to span the earth it is usual to use submarine
cables to extend one satellite link for antipodean connections. For some
data links using error-control that involves retransmission, delays of
0·5 second or more, that is loop delays exceeding a second, can be unacceptably large. Although nominally stationary, equatorial satellites do
have a small diurnal movement and the highly directional aerials used at
the ground stations have to be steered within one minute of arc to follow
their figure-of-eight path, and do so by tracking a radio beacon carried

31

by the satellite. Over long periods the satellite is perturbed by the gravitational attractions of the Sun and the Moon, and is corrected in orbit and attitude by gas thruster jets about once a year.

The carrier power that can be generated in a satellite is limited by the capacity of its solar cells to about 4 watts, and this combined with the long transmission path means that the received signal power is very small; very large receiving aerials of up to 30 metres diameter are therefore used at the earth stations. Current designs of satellite provide 10 or 12 bearer channels in each direction and each is capable of carrying several thousand telephone channels. These bearers can be switched by remote control between aerials having broader or narrower beams depending on whether a country or a continent is to be served. The use of satellite channels is doubling every 4 years and there is beginning to be the same kind of competition for a place in a geostationary orbit as there is for hilltops for ground links, and the same pressure is developing to use ever-higher carrier frequencies. The restriction arises not from any lack of space in space but because limitation of the size of the aerials that can be carried by the satellite implies limitation of their directivity, and so an increase in the minimum separation between adjacent satellites sharing the same frequency bands. Increasing the frequencies used will open up new and wider bands, and also make the aerials more directive, for this depends on their effective size measured in wavelengths. In combination, satellites and submarine cables can provide what in today's terms appears to be an unlimited number of channels at reasonable costs, and the volume of international communications is expanding rapidly and raising interworking problems that have already proved quite stubborn enough when confined within national systems. Satellites do have a potential role for domestic links also, especially for countries of large area, with remote unpopulous regions, or whose ground system is undeveloped: used for this purpose they would provide a system whose costs were independent of distance. Tests have shown satellite links to be very free from errors when used for data; some measured error rates being about 100 times lower than for land-based systems.

Waveguides and optical fibres

The problems of geographical clashes between competing microwave systems can be avoided by abandoning free-space propagation for transmission through a hollow copper pipe, or waveguide. The principle resembles that of the voice pipe, and the initial theoretical work was done by Lord Rayleigh in the last century. British development is concentrating on a cylindrical waveguide of about 50 mm diameter transmitting over the carrier frequency range 30 to 110 GHz. Such a guide can sustain several alternative modes of propagation, that is different patterns of electric and magnetic fields inside the guide; the circular

(TE$_{01}$) mode is used, and the guide is lined with a closely-wound helix of insulated copper wire to suppress all other modes. Unwanted modes of propagation are subject to higher attenuation than the TE$_{01}$ mode and travel at a different speed; when they are not suppressed they weaken the signal and give rise to echo distortion. A waveguide of this type should be able to carry 300 000 telephone channels, or data at 2000 Mbits/second. Its signal would need to be regeneratively amplified at intervals of 10 to 20 km, and a major disadvantage of existing designs is that they cannot be bent around sharp corners without transferring too much energy into unwanted modes. Restriction to bends of not less than 100 metres radius constrains the choice of route, although it would be possible to use railways and motorways which also need to be straight and which link the principal centres of population, and thus of data traffic. Waveguides must be precisely circular and be manufactured to very close tolerances on diameter and straightness, and there are some unsolved economic questions related to their jointing and repair in the field. When generators and amplifiers become available for frequencies above 100 GHz then, as well as opening up a further wide frequency band for exploitation, they will allow thinner and more flexible guides to be used and it may be possible to draw these into existing cable ducts.

At frequencies 100 000 times higher than microwaves, the 430 to 750 terahertz of visible light, an even wider frequency band would be entered by using laser technology for digital communication. Obviously, light signals would be disturbed by the weather and could be used only over short distances through the atmosphere, but they are not so limited in space. However, like electro-magnetic waves of lower frequencies, light can be guided through transparent rods. Two kinds of optical guide are under investigation. The first is designed to propagate a single mode and has a diameter comparable with the wavelength of light; it is encased in a fifty-times thicker coating which brings the total thickness up to that of a human hair. The second kind is some 20 to 100 times thicker and allows several different modes to coexist. Hollow silica fibres with liquid-filled cores are also being studied. Because they are thin and flexible a hundred or more optical fibres could be laid up together in one cable and pulled into existing ducts, and carry data at rates of 200 Mbits/second or more over each fibre. The economics of fibres depend on the attenuation of the light signals, for this will determine how close the repeaters must be. This attenuation depends on physical properties of the optical medium, and much work has been done on the production of extremely pure glasses. The costs of the repeaters and of the power and supervisory equipment will also be important, but it seems that optical fibres could become an economic alternative to coaxial cables when the signal energy reduction does not exceed 100 times per kilometre, and when data rates of 100 Mbits/second per fibre are achieved.

Their main application may prove to be for local distribution rather than inter-city trunks.

Concentrators

In each of the alternative systems reviewed the emphasis is on ever-wider bandwidth. There are two reasons for this. First, in practical data systems the delay experienced by a message depends more on the signalling rate—and thus on the bandwidth—than it does on the arrangement or lengths of the connections. Second, it is cheaper to provide one 100 MHz wide channel than 100 channels each 1 MHz wide; thus, at more mundane speeds the cost per bit transmitted is about three times higher for a 4·8 kbit/second channel than for a 48 kbit/second one. However, few data system applications require individual rates of 100 Mbit/second and signal combination and distribution are used to yield data rates of this order. Time-division multiplexing combines slow-speed channels into a single channel on an equal shares basis irrespective of whether a channel is active at the instant when its share falls due. When the number of channels is small, and their use sporadic, a 'Concentrator' may be used to combine only those channels that happen to be active, and by exploiting the statistics of demand it is possible to load more channels on to a single wideband channel by using a concentrator than by using a multiplexer. This advantage is won at the cost of more complex electronics. The sharply falling cost of small computers is bringing them into use as concentrators and communication controllers, for which purposes they offer considerable advantages. First, their data stores can be used to trap sharp peaks of traffic, and in this way allow the average signalling rate to be maintained at the maximum the channel allows, instead of well below it. Second, their stored program control can perform a very wide and flexible range of functions—it can, for example, temporarily inhibit particular channels when there happens to be a sustained peak in demand, and it can apply priorities in offering access to the wideband link.

Public networks

In travelling over a public telecommunications network a data signal may traverse an elaborate hierarchy of channels. [5] Consider, for instance, a possible route from the keyboard of a terminal to a distant computer centre:

(a) terminal sends 50 bits/second 'direct current' signals over a pair of wires to a local concentrator, where they combine with others;

(b) concentrator passes the combined signals to a local modem;

(c) modem translates the combined signal from the baseband into a frequency-modulated signal (1700 ± 500 Hz) at 500 bits/second which it sends over physical pairs to the local telephone exchange, where (*d*) the signal is extended over similar pairs in exchange junction cables to the nearest long-distance terminal, where

(*e*) it is multiplexed with other speech-band signals (telephone, telegraph and data) and

(*f*) the combined signal is sent over a wideband bearer channel to the distant long-distance terminal;

then follows (*g*), (*h*), (*i*), (*j*), (*k*), the inverse of (*e*), (*d*), (*c*), (*b*), (*a*). According to circumstances, the bearer channel of (*f*) could be one or more of: a small- or large-bore coaxial cable, a 2, 4, 6, or 11 GHz microwave link, a submarine coaxial cable or a 4 or 6 GHz satellite link.

The principal object of this chapter is to indicate that in passing through a typical public telephone system a data signal follows a complex sequence in which it undergoes many hidden transformations, and shares the use of many different kinds of link with a changing medley of other signals. All of these links are subject to secular change, to maintenance, to rearrangement, to extension, and to replacement. It is possible to take the view that all this is the business of the telecommunications authority, and that provided the stream of bits which emerges is indistinguishable from that which entered then the computer user need not concern himself with how this perfection is achieved. But this would be to ignore the inevitability of imperfection and the economics of error control, and to run the risk of suboptimization. Moreover, the needs of users differ in such matters as:

channel data speeds;

response time;

message length, code and format;

error control, detection and correction;

traffic volumes;

message priorities;

message sequence control, time and date recording;

message retrieval capability.

It is therefore essential that both the users and the authority be closely involved in establishing the requirements to be met when planning the development of data transmission. Fortunately the time is ripe, for after a period of little change today's rapid pace of technical advance is changing the economics of signal transmission, for example:

(*a*) by the use of LSI microelectronics to slash the sizes and costs and to boost the speeds of concentrators, multiplexers and modems, and so to tip the balance towards signal processing and against transmission path compensation as the best way to combat the effects of noise and distortion;

(*b*) by the increased reliability and reduced power consumption of repeaters using 'solid state' electronics, which makes it possible to widen the working bandwidth of coaxial—especially submarine—cables;

(c) by the drive to higher radio frequencies, thus opening up wider bands;
(d) by the very wide bands, free from mutual interference, offered by waveguides and optical fibres;
(e) by cheap wideband local distribution using small-bore coaxial or optical fibre cables, or millimetre radio links;
(f) by the integration that follows the use of digital techniques for multiplexing, transmission, and switching for both data and telephony.

These, and other, technical advances are facing telecommunications authorities with the need to choose between digital and analogue systems for telephony—a choice which is complicated by the merits of digital working for fully electronic switching in future exchanges. Nor are data and digital telephony the only new services to disturb the historic pattern of telecommunications; needs are also growing for various picture services such as visionphones, facsimile, and cable television. A considerable challenge to the established order is presented by the possibility of using satellites for internal as well as international links. A domestic satellite could provide a more complete geographical coverage than any existing national system, and do so without the immense labour of duplicating the present local and long-distance networks. However, the costs of establishing and maintaining a satellite service are very high, and the current need to have very large aerials at the ground stations would prevent their general use, quite apart from the rising competition for geostationary orbits. For these reasons it is inconceivable that the provision of data services by domestic satellite could ever be left wholly to uncontrolled private enterprise.

The matching of what is needed to what is available, or could be provided, is far from easy and there is rarely one best solution; this is a matter in which the computer user needs specialist telecommunications advice. It is easy to be misled by a superficial study, or by the results of an unrepresentative trial which takes insufficient account of the practical realities of operating a national telecommunication system—an operation in which the data customer is a latecomer, and troublesome far beyond his use of the system. Neither the telecommunications authority nor the data customer can afford to ignore the other. For the former, the rapid growth of data traffic poses a serious potential threat to his existing telephone and telegraph services, and especially to their long-term growth. For the latter, it would be folly indeed to overlook the unmatchable number and penetration of the outlets which the telephone network provides, or to forget that it is in the local distribution network that very heavy costs reside.

5

Making the right connections

In practical data systems it is not enough to transmit data from point to point: it is necessary also to make specified interconnections, for example, between a central computer and a few hundred remote terminals, none of which needs to be continuously connected. This requirement can be met by a private network of channels, by the ordinary telephone system—i.e. the public switched network, or by a packet switching system—public or private.

In most countries the responsibility for providing and operating telecommunication services is vested in one public authority which acts as a common carrier; in Britain this body is the Post Office, in some other European countries the P.T.T. In the U.S.A., a large number of commercial companies are authorized to act as common carriers but the scene is dominated by the two larger: the Western Union Telegraph Co; and the American Telephone and Telegraph Co. whose network is commonly called the Bell System. As well as providing public switched services these carriers lease channels for private use, which can be arranged and switched as the customer wishes.

Leased channels

Private networks using leased channels are used to link the branch offices of banks to their central computers, and to link the booking offices of airlines to their central seat reservation computers. They offer a number of advantages compared with the use of the public telephone system, for instance:

(a) they are cheaper when there is enough traffic to occupy the channel for more than a few hours each day during the peak rate period; the break-even point depends on the distance, the bandwidth, and the tariff structure of the country concerned;

(b) because the signal path is known and fixed they can be equalized to offset signal distortions and thus reduce the number of errors, or allow operation at higher data rates;

(c) the whole channel bandwidth is available for the customer's use without the need to leave room for the common carrier's own supervisory and control signals;

(d) there are fewer technical restraints of other kinds;

(e) careful routing can reduce the pick-up of switching and other impulse noise, thus reducing errors;

(f) they are less vulnerable to accidental overhearing;

(g) they are available instantly on demand without having to compete with other users;

(h) any data rate can be accommodated, up to the maximum that current technology makes possible.

But of course, no private network can match the telephone system's national and international coverage, or provide the opportunity to pay only for the time actually used in transmitting data.

Private networks can include duplicate links or alternative routes where it is important to protect the system against the failure of any connection. The layout of each network is an individual matter, and money can be saved by careful design. The designer does not have complete freedom, for the common carrier's plant is where it it and what it is, and not otherwise; his cables follow particular routes in the ground and the hill-tops used by his microwaves are where they are; but there are some general points that affect all networks. Common sense suggests that no two links should share the same bearer channel. Again, the most obvious way of linking several remote points to a central computer is by a star network (Fig. 5(a)), but then reliability can be increased only by the expensive duplication of each radial link—or at least of the more important or more vulnerable ones. As much reliability can be provided at less cost by linking the remote stations in a ring and joining the ring to the centre by three of four radial spokes (Fig. 5(b)); there is then, however, more risk of traffic congestion on the shared radials. Where economy is more important than reliability it is usual to reduce the number of radial links in a star system and use each to serve a string of terminals in a 'multi-drop' arrangement (Fig. 5(c)). This exploits the fact that few terminals, if any, are continuously active, and that even then their data rate is commonly much lower than the channel can carry. The disadvantage of a multidrop line is that on each radial only one terminal at a time can be active, and the cost of each terminal is increased by the need for it to be able to recognize a selective call, and also to identify itself. Total reliability is an unattainable ideal, and its needless pursuit expensive; for economic design it is important to determine what probability and duration of failure is acceptable.

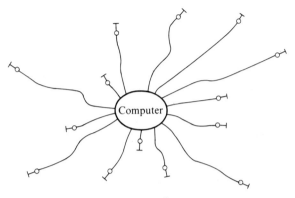

(a) Star network

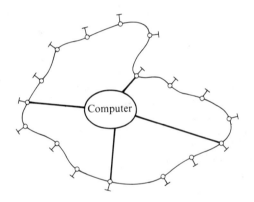

(b) Spoked wheel network

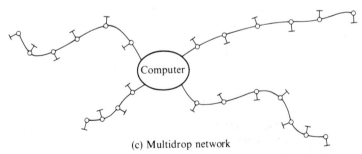

(c) Multidrop network

FIG. 5. Private network plans.

Network control

In network operation each computer can deal with only one data message at a time, and it is necessary to have some automatic means for responding in an orderly fashion to the demands presented by the terminals. Both logical and physical controls are needed and there are two broad approaches. In 'polling', the terminals are called selectively by the computer and asked if they have any data to send, or they have results sent to them. In 'contention mode', the terminals compete for service, calling for it when they require it and queueing when the demand is heavy. Network control is too mundane a function to occupy the time or the store of the main computer, and it is often cheaper to perform it either by a special-purpose communications controller, or by using a mini-computer programmed to behave as a controller, in which role it may be said to be 'front-ending' the main machine. The controller's task is to deal with the channels at the bit and character level, identifying them and delivering and receiving complete messages to and from the computer. It may be necessary for it to hold messages in queues, to handle priorities, to correct errors, to select routes and to keep a record of calls for traffic analysis and for charging. The controller requires a high-speed data store of some 32 to 256 kbytes, the size depending on the number of channels connected to it. The use of controllers is not confined to the centre; in a polling system where some channels are long ones cost can be reduced by using a controller to act as a message concentrator at a remote sub-centre by delegating to it the polling of the terminals in its vicinity and the relaying of their signals over a common link to the computer.

A concentrator, like a multiplexer, enables several data sources to share the same channel; but whereas the multiplexer combines several bit streams without changing them, the concentrator restructures the message or the bit pattern, for instance converting slow to fast or synchronous to asynchronous. Hence, it involves a store and forward action, which multiplexing does not. Message concentration is not solely used in private networks. In Britain, the Post Office offers a facility called Dataplex which allows a number of local calls over the public switched network to be combined on to one leased channel to a computer, so that for example a computer bureau or information service can be extended to a cluster of customers in a remote town without their having to dial and pay for more than a local call.

For data rates below about 10 kbits/second the public switched telephone network provides a versatile alternative to the use of private channels. It is ubiquitous, available on demand, charged by the use made, and cost effective. It is well suited to the sporadic activity which characterises so many remote computer applications, and is valuable also when a single terminal is used to obtain services from a number of alternative computer bureaux. This use of the network differs from that for which the telephone system was designed; a typical data call may last as long as 20 minutes and can last an hour, even though active transmission may occupy little more than one-third of that period—say 5 per cent from the terminal to the computer and 30 per cent in the reverse direction. This long 'holding time' of data calls means that a 200-line computer bureau can place as much load on its local exchange as 5000 residential telephone users, and thus generate severe problems of congestion.

Switching

In traversing the public telephone system a data message passes through the hierarchy of channels mentioned in Chapter 4, and also through a switching hierarchy. It is simplest to describe this in terms of one country but the same principle applies to all. In Britain then, the terminal launches its signals into a physical pair in one of the telephone cables to the local exchange—in Britain usually within 5 km, and one of 6000 similar exchanges. If the computer is also in the same locality the electro-mechanical switches in the exchange make the connection and the signal passes to the computer through similar local telephone cables. For more distant computers, the signal passes through more switches in a series of intermediate (tandem) exchanges that progressively route it to the nearest trunk exchange. In Britain this will be one of about 350 called 'Group Switching Centres', and at this point the signals enter the long-distance network over which they will be carried by one of the bearer channels already described. British Group Switching Centres are connected to 'District Switching Centres' (twenty-seven) and these in turn to 'Main Switching Centres' (nine). All main centres are connected to each other, as also are some district and group centres. District centres are connected to more than one main centre, and similarly group centres are connected to more than one district centre and also direct to main centres when one happens to be located nearby. In the worst case, a signal passing between the two group centres might have to traverse five intermediate links: group-district, district-main, main-main, main-district, and district-group; but in Britain less than 1 per cent of all calls have to do so, and about one-half of all calls use only three links.

In a system of this complexity an appreciable interval of time is needed to set up and clear down a long-distance call and this is a burdensome overhead for very brief messages, say for those shorter than a few thousands of bits. One way to overcome this disadvantage would be to establish a separate digital data network. This could share its transmission facilities (cables, microwaves and so on) with the telephone system, but would have its own local ends to data terminals and its own data switching exchanges. These could use improved techniques to give higher switching speed and greater reliability for they would not have to be compatible with the older exchanges of the telephone system. Again, present networks suffer limitations from the use of the same channel to carry the data signals and the supervisory and control signals used to set up, clear down, and charge for the call; a new network could use separate channels for these purposes, which would increase the speeds of set up and also of data transmission. In such a network the special local ends might work synchronously at rates from 600 to 9600 bits/second into the local telephone exchange where they would be multiplexed with others over a 64 kbits/second data link to the nearest data exchange. The data exchanges would be interconnected with each other by, say, 2 Mbits/second links, and the whole could be designed to keep the total set up time below one second, and the error below 1 per 10 million bits.

Packet switching

The development and rising popularity of computer systems in which business and professional men, workshop foremen and managers, and other amateurs of the keyboard use remote terminals at 10 to 20 bits/ second to interrogate a central computer or to report data to it, has attracted attention to the very inefficient use of the data channel which this brings, and has led to the design of an alternative method which switches data messages rather than data channels. Several broadly similar methods have been proposed, with such titles as 'store and forward', 'message switching', and 'packet switching'. They are all developments of the automatic methods used to route telegraph messages, and offer a kind of fast electronic equivalent to the postal service. Of the three terms mentioned, the last two are almost synonymous, and are often used as if they were, but they differ in that message switching handles complete messages of whatever length they happen to have (up to a stated maximum), whereas packet switching handles all messages in 'packets' of a standard length. The first term is also used as a loose synonym, but whether it is so depends on the capacity and facilities associated with the storage function. Packet switching need not involve very much storage, but a store-and-forward system could, for example, accumulate and store reports from local branches as these trickle in during the day and forward them in bulk by night when the channels are free and the charges are low.

In packet switching the data signals pass from a terminal bit by bit, or character by character over physical pairs to a local 'packet-switching exchange' where they are assembled into packets each of which, for instance, might comprise:

(*a*) a control header which indicates the type of message, its length, its serial number, and the delivery response, charging and other facilities required, plus a label identifying the sending terminal or computer, say 48 bits altogether;

(*b*) a destination address indicating the receiving computer or terminal, say 32 bits;
(*c*) one packet's worth of the data message, say 2048 bits;
(*d*) error check characters, say polynomial code check 16 bits.

The packet switching exchanges will also accept messages in the standard packet form from high-speed terminals or from computers.

The exchange validates the label by identifying the terminal as a registered, paid-up user of the system. It selects the appropriate route for the message, holds it until the route is free and then launches it forwards to the next exchange where its destination address is examined and the message forwarded if the required route is free, or diverted to a queue if it is busy, or to an alternative route if the delay is likely to be excessive. This process of scrutiny and forwarding is repeated until the addressed destination is reached. Each successive exchange examines the check characters on arrival, invokes retransmission as necessary, and will not forward an incorrect message. Over the main high-speed links between exchanges packets from different terminals are interleaved, thus allowing a flexible, automatic allocation of link capacity and closer packing of the traffic than is possible under the more rigid operations of time division multiplexing, in which the time slot is made available whether it can be fully utilized or not. The final exchange 'opens' the packet and delivers its data content to the named terminal at whatever rate that terminal can absorb it. All this may seem to be a lengthy process, but it should normally be completed in a small fraction of a second. Such a system has been established in the U.S.A. by the Advanced Projects Research Agency (ARPA), and in it the average packet delay is 0·2 second. The delay varies with the traffic volumes on the routes actually followed by the packet, and rises rather rapidly when congestion begins to build up queues.

The advantages claimed for packet switching include:
(*a*) high utilization of the links by interleaving packets from independent sources to fill the gaps, hence fewer channels required by a computer centre;
(*b*) lower costs due to those fewer channels, and also to the reduced need for multiplexers and modems;
(*c*) data rate and code matching between different terminals and computers, synchronous or asynchronous;
(*d*) simplified control equipment and procedures from the use of fewer, high-density, links and a common message format;
(*e*) link-by-link error protection to a specified high standard, say 1 per 10 million bits;
(*f*) reliability by automatic re-routing when intermediate links fail, packet switching exchanges may be fully interconnected or triangulated;

(g) automatic redistribution of traffic or priorities to relieve congested links or exchanges when queues develop;

(h) automatic system fault detection by means of frequent test messages over all links;

(i) priority routing, queue jumping, and handling;

(j) the ability to send even when the receiving terminal is busy or out of order, re-routing to named alternative destinations;

(k) the ability to deposit data for delayed delivery, say to match timezone differences;

(l) privacy protection by automatic restraints on the addresses to which an exchange will route packets from specified terminals, so that a closed group of users can be formed within a public system;

(m) logging of messages on tape for audit trail;

(n) broadcast facilities;

(o) format error detection, for example of invalid addresses or indicators;

(p) message processing is possible, for instance code conversion, file reformatting, automatic addressing based on message content, message and packet numbering, dating and timing, traffic statistics for network utilization studies.

This long list of the virtues that have been claimed for packet switching has a somewhat self-righteous air, reminiscent of a sales brochure. Many of the claimed advantages are not specific to packet switching—for example, (e), (f), (h), (l), (m), (n), and (o) could be included in any network specifically designed for data transmission, especially when small computers are used for network control. Amid this mass of claims it is important to recall what may be said for channel switching:

(a) it is well proved by years of practice;

(b) it is cheaper than packet switching for the same traffic load;

(c) it is better for long messages, for which its set-up overhead is incurred once only, whereas every packet-switching exchange processes every character in every message;

(d) modern techniques could provide faster set up than packet switching, and constant transmission time—which are better for real-time use;

(e) successive messages, or parts of the same message, cannot arrive out of sequence due to variable routing and queueing;

(f) the system is code-transparent and format-transparent, for it transmits data as a stream of bits at any speed up to its design limit;

(g) analogue signals can be handled if necessary.

Packet system costs and charges

Some computer users appear to entertain rather innocent expectations about the lower costs of using a packet switching system, which they base on their own sporadic usage and a strong sense of natural justice which leads them to feel they should pay only for the occasional brief intervals when they are actually transmitting data over the system and not, as in channel switching, for their total 'connect time'. Clearly this happy state could not arrive until the system was in full use and bearing an economic load, for the costs of establishing and operating it are almost completely independent of the traffic carried. These costs would have to be carried by those, few or many, who chose to use the system, unless they were to be subsidized by other customers of the telecommunications authority. Different authorities may well take different views about such a subsidy, depending on their financial criteria; some could be instructed to subsidize the infant data service on social grounds, others could decide to do so as a speculative investment intended to build a potentially profitable future market. Clearly, no such subsidy would be possible in a separately-owned network. Data users have also expressed views about the structure of the charges for data transmission; they would for example, like to pay in proportion to the total number of bits they transmit, irrespective of the speed or distance travelled. But, the costs of a packet switching system do depend on the lengths and bandwidths of the links, and on the sizes and speeds of the stores in the exchanges—for these determine the queueing time. It seems likely that in a packet switching system the charges will be based on the identified and timed use of the exchanges and the links and other shared equipment, and on the full-time use of exclusive equipment such as the user's local connection; and it is naïve to suppose that the high coasts of the shared equipment will permit low charges until there is sufficient traffic to keep it busy. Incidentally, such a method of charging would involve the keeping of records of the passage of every message through every exchange, thus leaving a clear trace of an individual's use of the system and opening up further problems related to the protection of privacy.

The economic design of a packet switching network is obscure: too generously designed it could be very costly; but too meanly designed it could run into serious problems of congestion when the traffic approached the design limit; the analysis of queueing in a multi-path network is complex, and the operating rules for dealing with untoward events far from easy to formulate in the absence of experience. In Britain, the Post Office is to conduct a trial of an experimental packet system for public use in order to acquire the information needed to propose operating standards and practices, to determine an economic set of facilities, and to establish a reasonable pattern of charges. The situation is very plastic, but channel switching and packet switching could have complementary roles to play in the telecommunication networks of the future. Neither system is clearly better than the other in all circumstances. Channel switching may be better for dealing with long messages, high traffic densities and real-time systems. Packet switching may be more useful as a public system used for brief interrogatory messages, for occasional users, and for offering access from any telephone to a wide range of computing and information services.

The only defensible reason for excluding packet switching from consideration would be to avoid the diversion of resources from the channel switching systems needed for the main business of the telephone authorities. In Europe these authorities are facing the prospect of continuing rapid growth of data traffic over the same period as they face large programmes of expansion and re-equipment of their telephone systems, programmes which will impose unprecedented demands on their financial and human resources, and on the manufacturing capacity of their suppliers. Their problems are further complicated by the coincidence that this is a time of rapid technological change arising from the invention of the transistor. Such changes resemble the eruptions of volcanoes; both are infrequent, unheralded, expensive, and change the affected landscape. In telecommunications, transmission engineers have to decide how far and how fast to introduce digital systems; switching engineers have to decide how and when their electro-mechanical dinosaurs should give way to electronic exchanges: matters would be vastly simpler for both if the telecommunications system were totally digital and if no old equipment existed. In reality, innovation has to come to terms with the enormous investments of the past and the outcome must be evolution not revolution. The important thing is to make certain that the telecommunication authorities take data seriously as an increasingly important sector of their future markets—and not one so far in the future that nothing need to be done about it today.

Some have used these difficulties to construct a case for taking data out of the telephone systems, arguing that neither the authorities nor their traditional suppliers have adjusted themselves to the recent rapid pace of technical advance, and that they are not likely to divert sufficient resources away from what they still see as their main business. We shall need to return to this point in Chapter 8, but it is worth noting the increasing strength of the computer manufacturers as a pressure group; they could wish to seek out new areas of business as they approach saturation of their original market—and they have the right combination of resources to enter telecommunications. They may, moreover, prefer to deal with individual private network operators drawn from the group of customers they already know rather than take on the entrenched might of the telephone administrations and the long-established telecommunications suppliers, and it would not be surprising if they were to enter the lists on the private side.

6

Face to face

In communicating with computers the most important requirement is that *we* should be able to communicate with them to ensure that they accept our data and obey our commands, and produce their results in ways that suit us, and not in ways dictated by limitations of their design. There are problems at two levels. First, and simpler, we have the engineering problems of exchanging data between our minds and computer stores; these are the problems of terminal hardware design involving electronics, ergonomics, and economics. Second, and very much more difficult, we have the stubborn conceptual problems associated with organizing, processing, and presenting information in the ways we find congenial; these are the systems and software problems.

Computer terminals

For the first-level problems solutions will be produced more by market forces than by anything else, for they depend mainly on the completion of straightforward development work, and its pace and timing will depend on the effort which the suppliers of equipment think it worthwhile to apply. Today's most popular instruments for data input and output are keyboard machines of one kind or another, in particular the electric typewriters on computer consoles and the teleprinters and teletypes used remotely. These machines were designed for quite different purposes and, at 10 characters per second, they print too slowly to keep up with a computer's output or to read as it comes. Hence, when a printed record (hard copy) is not required the printing mechanism can be replaced by a video display unit (VDU) which presents the text on a television screen by using electronic circuits to generate the outlines of some specified set of characters. A typical VDU displays 1000 to 2000 characters simultaneously, for example as 25 lines each of 80 characters, and it has facilities for tabulation, indexing, erasure, and the display of fixed information for format control.

Visual display units are often designed to meet the needs of one particular application; even so they commonly have a standard typewriter keyboard—although typing skills are not widespread and the layout is far from ideal—plus some additional keys for signalling commands for some of the more frequently used functions. As adaptations of a general-purpose design they cannot pretend to achieve a complete ergonomic match to the abilities and limitations of the intended set of users in relation to the speed, accuracy, and volume requirements of their system.

And, although their displays are much less frustrating to read than the plodding print-out of a standard teleprinter, the cathode-ray tubes of many VDUs leave much to be desired in respect of clarity, brilliance, and freedom from flicker, and can induce fatigue in their operators and lead to errors. Again, when a large volume of output has to be examined it has to be scanned by scrolling, and peering through a small moving window is a tiresome nuisance. The input speed of a VDU is set by the competence of its keyboard operator, but its output speed can be very much faster, and VDUs place a highly asymmetric demand on the channel linking them to the computer, say 50 bits/second inwards and 8000 bits/second outwards.

An important advantage of providing computing services through remote terminals is to promote their direct and frequent use by engineers, clerks, managers, salesmen, and others in the ordinary course of their daily work. This means that these unskilled keyboard operators will be replacing trained professionals with adverse effects on both speed and accuracy, and the computer system designer has to pay much more attention to 'vetting' the input data so that bloomers can be detected and corrected at the moment of entry. The economics of the system must be able to bear the processing overhead which this additional data vetting incurs. However, because the vetting program challenges the errors as they occur by returning a query to the terminal, and the revised entry is then considered by someone for whom the data have meaning—as opposed to being just one more page of copy—the final result may well be a reduction rather than in increase in the number of errors.

Data input and output rates can be increased by working off-line, for example by using keyboard machines to punch holes in paper tape or cards or to record directly on magnetic tapes or discs which are then batched for later input by fast automatic machines connected to the computer. Similarly, the computer can print its results a line at a time, and 10 or 20 lines per second, on a continuous roll of paper which is subsequently cut and collated for human perusal. The word 'line' is singularly misleading in this context for it does not refer to the use of a telegraph or telephone line. For the input, 'off-line' means operating with the keyboard not directly controlled by the computer; that is 'line' has the sense of a production line. For the output, 'line-printer' is an abbreviation for 'line-at-a-time-printer', as opposed to a typewriter which in this terminology is a 'character-printer'. Where large volumes of data flow to and from a remote point, a card reader and a line printer may be installed there and work to the computer over a telecommunications channel in a method of operation known as 'remote job entry' (RJE). Typical data rates for paper-tape or punched-card readers, and for line printers, fall in the range 1000 to 2000 characters/second; say 8000 to 20 000 bits/second.

Intelligent terminals

A different kind of terminal is used for graphical data, which arise for example in meteorology, medicine, engineering and architectural design, and air-traffic control. In the most common method the operator uses a photo-sensitive stylus (light pen) to identify a point on a television display. Its coordinates are then automatically recorded by the associated computer. In this way a list is built up in the computer's store of the data that describe the diagram, and the computer has the ancillary, housekeeping, task of re-presenting the data to the screen several times a second in order to refresh and up-date the display: this housekeeping is no small task, and together with other routine functions—say, drawing a straight line or an arc of a circle to pass through specified points—it may be delegated to a cheaper mini-computer associated with the display. Such a terminal having delegated functions, is what is meant by an 'intelligent terminal'. The term is unfortunate, for the terminal's behaviour is produced by a very restricted set of totally determinate conditioned responses, with no learning or exploratory capability, but as it is now inescapable the word 'intelligent' should always in this context be imagined to be disinfected by quotation marks.

When an intelligent terminal is used the main computer is reserved for the principal computation, the data flow between it and the terminal is much reduced, and a cheaper, narrower-band channel can be employed. There is also some saving of the main computer's time, but since it is widely claimed that large computers are more cost-effective than small ones this should yield no cash saving—indeed, whether it is worth-while depends on what alternative use can be made of the time so saved. Any savings are offset by the cost of the mini-computer, and the economic balance depends on the current costs of telecommunications and of small computers. At present, mini-computer costs are falling faster than telecommunications costs, and they remain under the user's control for the life of the computer, with the hope that their replacement will be cheaper; hence, the distance beyond which it pays to use an intelligent terminal is decreasing. Intelligent terminals are not restricted to graphical data; they can be used for remote job entry and could become almost universal when the predicted dramatic fall in the price of mini-computers is realized. As well as economy, they offer great scope for increasing the convenience of communicating with computers, which at present requires rather too many concessions by men to the stupidity of machines. There are, however, some possible risks. Thus intelligent terminals and other forms of disseminated computing power could be used to validate, condense, re-arrange, and generally pre-edit the input of data in a large system, and do so with considerable economic advantage. But, this implies that some data would be rejected, and all data would be processed, and so that one particular interpretation would be imposed *before* the data were presented for anlaysis or recording. In most routine applications this would not be troublesome, but as information engineering systems become more flexible and more pervasive it could prove to be dangerous to force them into blinkers in this way.

Standardization

Developments in micro-electronic technology now make it possible to manufacture a powerful data processor on a single chip of silicon, and the implications of chips with everything are extremely significant. Many tiresome problems connected with national and international standardization would disappear if single-chip processors were freely scattered throughout information engineering systems to match and convert from one set of standards to another. If we can use electronic converters between different colour television standards, data conversions should present little technical difficulty; and as costs continue to fall it may well become cheaper to convert than to attempt to harmonize. As well as saving much time and patience this would avoid the major disadvantage of standardization, namely, limiting our freedom of design, for these are such early days in this field that it would be foolish to impose any unnecessary restraints on innovation. Single-chip electronics is also being used in the pocket calculators which are sweeping away the clumsier electro-mechanical desk models; their extension to stored-program control, the addition of cassette tapes for data and program storage—including standard reference data and library programs, and their linking to domestic television screens for display will allow them to assume many functions that would otherwise have provided work for terminals connected to remote computers. The introduction of miniature electronic circuits is producing a Hegelian sequence of development, thus: thesis, large-scale integrated circuits produce antithetical developments of (a) much larger computers (because their greater reliability allows more complex computer systems to be constructed) and (b) much smaller computers (because a complete mini-computer can be made on a single silicon chip): and these issue in a synthesis in which mini-computers control intelligent terminals connected to large central machines.

Some terminal developments

Data are also being collected by means of portable electronic notebooks consisting of a keyboard and a tape-cassette recorder. A typical

cassette holds about 500 000 characters and can be sent to the computer
by courier or by post, or its data can be replayed over a 2400 bits/second
link. These 'data capture' devices could be used by gas and electricity
meter readers, but alternatively the existing meters could be replaced
by micro-electronic chips able to measure, record, and transmit their
readings over a telephone line either on demand or on schedule, for
example at cheap night rates when the channels are idle. Here again, the
technical problems are straightforward and the outcome will be determined by weighing the wage costs of human meter readers against the
costs of their redundandancy and of displacing the enormous existing
investment in mechanical meters. This example, and the previous one of
the pocket calculator, reveal the existence of unresolved alternatives
which add to the many difficulties of forecasting the growth of demand
for data transmission services.

Cheap and really portable data terminals would allow travelling salesmen to interrogate their firm's computers about stocks and deliveries,
and to register orders. Clearly they need access from any telephone with
as little formality as possible. This requirement has led to the development of 'acoustic couplers' which generate the data signals as sequences
and combinations of audio tones emitted by a small loudspeaker placed
near the microphone of the telephone handset. These couplers are
obviously interim devices for use until all telephones are fitted with a
socket for the direct connection of data terminals and other information
engineering equipment. A socket could be used to draw a small amount
of power from the telephone exchange battery to operate the electronic
circuits in the terminal, and specifications have been formulated. Some
commentators have welcomed this as a major advance, but it is difficult
to believe that 'line-powered' terminals will be used in many situations
where neither dry batteries nor mains power are available, for something
must be used to run the lighting! Acoustic couplers are not loved by the
telephone authorities because they are inefficient and vulnerable to room
noise; moreover their widespread use could lead to attempts to impose
constraints on future designs of telephone. But direct connection also
poses worrying problems, for the authorities themselves use parts of the
voice band for setting up, clearing down, and charging for the call and
there are possibilities of interference. Again, metallic interconnection
demands strict standards of electrical safety; and the signal power and
spectrum must each be limited in order to avoid interference to other
users of the telephone system. Line-powered terminals would have no
safety problem, and could control the maximum signal power by limiting
the power drawn from the line. All of this implies a considerable measure
of standardization and regulation which has tended to give the authorities
a surly dog-in-the-manger image that they did not, in this instance,
deserve.

A potentially large group of data terminals involves human beings only indirectly. These include telemetry devices for meteorological data, for monitoring the activity of gas and electricity distribution networks, for measurements of river flow, for pollution control, and for traffic observation and control. There is also a large group of point-of-sale recorders, for example supermarket cash registers, transport and sport turnstile recorders, and in future, perhaps, vehicle identifiers to collect data for charging differentially for road use. The really large market awaits the development of domestic uses for data terminals, and these are easy enough to imagine. The problems of user familiarization and of investment, each on a mass scale, make it likely that this market will be built on the use of the telephone dial (by then a set of 12 push buttons) with the response spoken, or displayed on the home television screen: dialled interrogation and spoken response is already in use. It is impossible to foresee how soon or how fast such services may develop, but there are prophets eager to predict the arrival of the 'wired city' in which every office and every house will be connected to information and computing systems. Spoken output is easy; it merely requires the automatic selection of pre-recorded phrases or the controlled generation of speech sounds. Spoken input is a commonplace of science fiction but it presents exceedingly severe technical problems because we speak with very few constraints on pitch, loudness, rate and clarity of articulation, accent, vocabulary, or syntax. The solution of the speech-recognition problem in general terms, as opposed to dealing with the nursery vocabularies now available, may well provide a rather striking illustration of how to mop up the enormous computing power which advances in electronics are now putting into our hands, and become a paradigm of conspicuous waste for sociologists to use when discussing the behaviour of the post-industrial world.

Widespread access to computer systems from remote terminals over a public telecommunications network raises questions of security and integrity, and protection will be needed against unauthorized use, whether accidental, frivolous, or fraudulent. Protection against trespassers implies sensible use of physical controls over access to terminals by lock, key, password, and identity card. Some systems use plastic cards with an embedded magnetic recording which is read by the terminal and sent to be checked by the called computer before it will accept a request for service. The same card can be used to define the range or class of service to be given, and as a credit card in billing for it. The use of automatic finger-print readers, the analysis of speech characteristics (voice-prints), or of trace elements in a hair, or of the chemical 'signature' of bodily secretions have all been suggested as identifiers and some of them are providing great intellectual interest to their investigators. The problem is not entirely technical, for it has a substantial element of war gaming. Absolute protection is not possible; as in the design of bank vaults, the rational approach is to seek to discourage the amateur and delay the professional to some specified degree. It is easy to be tempted into cleverness when designing a protective method, but if it is too cumbersome for the authorized users it will simply be circumvented by them. Moreover, criminals are unlikely to desert their well-proved methods of corrupting the weak or sensitive employee: great technical subtlety is much more likely to be practised as a sport by mischievous amateurs, committed as a nuisance by disgruntled employees, or brought to the aid of sabotage by injured consumers or self-styled anarchists.

Some conceptual problems

Progress towards solutions for the second-level conceptual problems of communicating with computers is likely to remain slow and uncertain, for it waits on good ideas in linguistics and classification, fields which are littered with unsolved problems and haunted by the spirits of problems yet unborn. Here we can do no more than make sufficient money available to support any work that offers progress, and this will demand a sustained act of faith, for the intended research is bound to appear to be impracticably academic, no result can be guaranteed, and it may be very difficult to assess either the merit of what is proposed or the value of what has been achieved. We are still in the pre-scientific or natural history stage of this subject, and it must be a long time before we can hope to lay a firm foundation for the construction of information systems.

One important subset of the problems of the second level concerns the languages we use for instructing computers. At the highest level we have the 'command language' employed by the user of some specific system to initiate the performance of its standard functions. The structure of a system's command language is entirely within the control of its designer, but because he is more often a computer expert than an expert in the application area there is a communication problem between him and the prospective users, and a risk that his command language may be convenient and elegant for the computer rather than relevant, effective, and acceptable to the men who will use it. One of the benefits we may hope to reap from the increasing power and decreasing costs of computers is being able to divert more of their capacity away from the main computation, and applying it to making our communication with them more helpful to us.

At the more detailed level of programming, we have the problem of matching the precise but myopic step-by-step action of a computer in terms of a small set of elementary operators to our broader but rather fuzzy conceptual thinking. At present we have to attempt this task with general-purpose programming languages, of which Algol, Fortran, Cobol, and PL/1 are the better known. A general-purpose language must be a compromise, with artificial restraints on vocabulary and format, but many are also guilty of arbitrariness and are deficient logically, and all this makes their effective use a matter of detailed training and continuous practice; they are hazardous and unsuitable for the kind of sporadic use that ordinary men and women would like to make of computers. The aim must be to allow architects and engineers, salesmen and statisticians, doctors and social workers each to use the concepts of his own speciality, rather than having to recast his thinking into the rigid mould of some general-purpose language of which the best that can be said is that it is no worse for any one than for any other. A solution may lie in the use of microprogramming, for this allows the instruction repertoire of a computer to be changed; it could perhaps be developed to the point where a computer could have a library of interchangeable microprograms so that it could be set up to obey any of a number of specialist programming languages directly or interpretatively.

Modems

There can be little doubt that where man confronts machine across their common interface is where the biggest challenge lies in communicating with computers. This is not an area that raises many problems of engineering policy, partly because it is so impoverished technically that there is rarely an opportunity for choosing between alternatives. The principal issue of current interest concerns the supply and maintenance of terminals, and arises from the split of responsibilities between the terminal manufacturer, the computer manufacturer, and the telecommunications authority, with the consequent risk that the user's interest in good performance overall may slip down one or other of the cracks between them. In many respects the telecommunications authority, with its national force of installation and maintenance technicians, is best placed to supply and maintain the terminals as well as the channels, but it would obviously wish to confine its responsibility to those models that it had tested and approved, and would probably want to limit the number of different designs in order to reduce the variety of spares and the volume of training. Such a limitation would be considered by many computer men to apply an unacceptably heavy brake to progress. The terminal problem is inevitably linked with that of the modem, for if the two were to be combined then circuits, space, and cost could be saved. Telecommunication authorities see modems as a part of their systems, arguing that they are better placed than anyone else to provide designs which match the particular—and changing—circumstances of their plant. To computer system designers this appears to be a purely defensive reflex; indeed, the more cynical of them have observed that improved modems would increase the rate of flow of data through a given channel and reduce the revenue earned by the transmission of a given number of bits. It is probably nearer to the truth to say that the authorities genuinely doubt whether computer men really understand the practical engineering problems presented by systems which, because they have evolved over many decades, contain a wide variety of equipment with a wide range of ages and a broad and changing spread of performance characteristics. It is true to say, also, that the authorities have been accustomed to provide telecommunication services to customers who have taken no interest in the technical means by which this was accomplished; they are now slightly shocked to find themselves in the position of a restaurateur whose latest customers wish to poke around in his kitchen, and not simply to enjoy the food. In the 'touch-tone' (push-button) telephone 'dial' we have a terminal which avoids many of the problems: it does not require a modem, it is line-powered, it is designed, provided and maintained by the authority; and in conjunction with an automatically-spoken response it could become the most ubiquitous instrument for communicating with computers.

The real meaning of real time

7

A fully-interactive, multi-access, time-sharing, on-line, real-time computer system—the hyphenated adjectives roll off the tongue like the name of a fine German wine; but what does it all mean? These terms tend to be used interchangeably, but they are quite distinct and confusion can occur unless their context removes all ambiguity.

Interactive

Thus, 'fully-interactive' means that the course of the computer's operation is being closely directed by its user's responses to the results which it is presenting to him in a kind of dialogue between man and machine; indeed, 'conversational working' is a common synonym for this way of working. The data used, the programs employed and the choices between alternative routes through them, are moulded by the user to suit his requirements as these in turn are shaped by the computation. An information system, for example, can guide an enquirer by responding to the answers he gives to a set of questions designed to narrow its field of search. Many benefits are claimed for interactive working. By challenging obvious bloomers and entries of doubtful credibility an interactive data-vetting program can trap most of the errors generated by the unskilled use of keyboards by clerks and managers, statisticians and scientists, in the ordinary course of their work. Similarly, when an interactive terminal is being used for writing a program the computer rejects for immediate correction those silly little errors of spelling, punctuation, and syntax that can waste so much time and mental effort during program testing: errors of this sort also, are more frequent when non-expert users write their occasional programs. Interactive working returns the user to the driving seat from which he has far too long been ousted by specialist analysts and programmers—a circumstance which has caused many problems in communicating with computers.

Multi-access, time-sharing

'Multi-access' means simply that the system is serving many remote
terminals independently; one method of achieving this is by 'time-
sharing' which is a mode of operation where several separate programs
run together in one computer. Their operation is sometimes said to be
simultaneous, but is more correctly called concurrent, for at any one
instant the computer can execute only one instruction drawn from one
of the sharing programs. The process resembles time-division multiplexing and various methods are used to allocate the computer's time; thus,
it may be parcelled into 'slots' or 'slices' of equal duration and each
program given its turn in rotation. Alternatively, time may be allocated
on demand in sufficient amount to complete some unit of work, or in
accordance with pre-set priorities. Time-sharing is common in large
commercial batch processing installations, for in these the throughput
is choked back by their slow electro-mechanical peripheral equipments
and a single central computer can keep more of these fully occupied
than can be deployed on a single program. But, even when only one user
program is being run the operation of a large computer is controlled by
its operating system software, and its time is therefore being divided between this master program and its user's work.

On-line

The previous chapter notes that 'on-line' does not mean 'connected
to a telecommunications line' but 'under direct control by the computer'.
Thus, the card readers, printers, magnetic tape decks, discs, and drums
and other peripheral devices installed in the computer room operate on-
line, for if they did not the speed of processing would be quite hopelessly
cut down to that of human responses to signals arising within the program.
Interactive terminals also must work on-line and because they are intended
to serve their users at their normal places of work they usually involve
operation at the end of a data link; this mode of working is also known
as 'teleprocessing'. Remote on-line operation is considerably more expensive than local batch processing not only by reason of the added telecommunication costs, but also because the requests made by a population
of independent terminal users are more varied and more sporadic than
those of local peripheral devices all working to a single program; hence,
a substantial proportion of the computer's time is deflected into housekeeping tasks associated with the control of communications and the
location, marshalling, and storage of data and programs. As communication and computing costs continue to fall the surcharge imposed by
the housekeeping overhead is becoming less significant, and there are
already many circumstances in which remote on-line working is attractive, and some in which it is justifiable; thus:

(*a*) multi-access interactive working for scientific computing, engineering design, information services, program development, and so on;
(*b*) other situations in which uneven or unpredictable loading make it impossible to schedule batch processing;
(*c*) small-scale demand for services which can be more economically provided by the shared use of a large central computer;
(*d*) the use of shared computer files ('common data bases') as a means of internal communication and coordination in a large organization;
(*e*) networking, that is serving a group of users from several alternative computers in order to make a wider range of programs or data available, to allow peaks of work to be off-loaded, or to cover breakdowns;
(*f*) imperative need for up-to-date information or quick action, as in industrial automation, traffic control, and some telemetry;
(*g*) similar to (*f*), but the collection and distribution of data where the aim is economy and convenience rather than quick collection, as in domestic meter reading.

Each of these circumstances can vary widely in its quantitative requirements, for instance (*c*) can range from the use of a single keyboard terminal up to 'Remote Job Entry' (RJE) in which non-urgent data and programs are loaded at a remote point for subsequent processing and the return of results.

Cost and time

It is worth digressing at this point to note that there are many situations in which a telecommunications link is used to convey data between a computer and a distant user without either on-line or interactive working being involved. Indeed, most computers *are* remote from their end-users, being concealed in air-conditioned rooms and encircled by specialist attendants. When, as is commonly the case for the computer systems of national companies, the computer is far away from most of its data sources it is important to consider all alternative methods of data communication. When time is critical a telecommunications link is indicated, but it is necessary to remember that while telecommunications delivers the nose of a message almost immediately its tail follows much later when the message is long and the channel narrow. For large amounts of data, or where overnight delivery is adequate, the old-fashioned technologies of postal and courier services become competitive in cost; and they have the further advantage of being free from error (except when they lose the lot, which is rare and an easy situation to handle); they are moreover completely private (apart from the unlikely, and then obvious, circumstances of robbery). No example can hope to do more than give the very roughest illustration of relative costs and speeds, for the particulars are bound to be different at different times and in different places and so much depends on the basic assumptions, but three (admittedly extreme) examples are given in Table 7.1 to emphasize the point, for it tends to be overlooked.

TABLE 7.1

Comparative costs and speeds for 100 miles (160 km)

Message length	Telecommunications (at 2400 bits/second)		Post or courier
(characters)	Cost times the post or courier cost	Time for complete delivery	Time for complete delivery (hours)
100	0·3	0·33 second	24 (post)
500 000[1]	1·5	28 minutes	24 (post)
50 000 million[2]	500	2000 days	5 (own van)[2]

[1] One full magnetic tape cassette.
[2] One van fully loaded with high-density magnetic tapes.

These examples are less than fair to telecommunications, for they cost the postal and courier services under their most advantageous loading conditions; and the third example is somewhat unreal. Nor do they allow for the exploitation of cheap night rate transmission of bulk data when the telecommunication network is otherwise idle. Nevertheless they demonstrate that it makes little sense to ship extremely large amounts of data from point to point over telecommunication channels, for in the third example even a coaxial cable having 3000 times the capacity of the telephone channel assumed in the example would still be slower than the courier, and a good deal more expensive. The special merit of telecommunications is its capability for collecting or distributing small quantities of data very quickly to and from a large number of remote points, rather than in the carriage of a large quantity between two fixed points.

When considering the significance of the time needed to convey data it is important to look also at the total situation. For example, a three-day input cycle is not unknown in commercial computing, because the preparation of the data is often batched in order to load the operators and their machines efficiently, thus:

Day 1. Data entered on forms and sent to punch room.
Day 2. Cards punched and verified.
Day 3. Input to computer; data vetting program lists queries for return to punch room for check and correction.

Real-time

'Real-time' was first applied when an analogue computer was being used to model the behaviour of some physical system, and it denoted the special case in which the model 'operated' at the same speed as the modelled real world system. Transferred to the wider context of digital computing, real-time now indicates a computer system that is fast enough to keep up with the external events it is being used to monitor or control, and which accepts and deals with data about these events as and when they occur. For example, an air-traffic control computer must take in and process data from radars and pilots as these data arrive, or at any rate soon enough to generate the results needed to inform the air-traffic controllers. The essence of real-time working is rapid, on-demand response to external stimuli. Clearly, real-time systems imply on-line operation, and usually remote on-line, but not vice versa. Paradoxically, the rapid response of a real time system reduces the pressure on its user, for it allows him to work at his own pace rather than rushing to meet an imminent decision, or to catch the deadline of a batch-processing schedule.

The time-scale appropriate to the response depends on the application and must not be dictated by accidents of the computer's design. To be economic in design and use the system should operate in the time-scale relevant to the real need of the real user, and few users need so fast a reaction as air-traffic control. Thus, in descending order of speed we have:

(*a*) the automatic control of traffic, vehicles, weapons, or industrial plant, and the automatic routing of telecommunications messages; responses are required within a few milliseconds or less, for the actions which follow are those of high-speed machines, and only the general direction of events is regulated by the slower responses of men;

(*b*) on-demand seat-reservation systems require a response acceptable to a booking clerk confronted by a queue, and although none of his customers is likely to worry about waiting for a few seconds the clerk needs a rapid reassurance that the system is still working and has accepted his request as a valid one; 1 or 2 seconds is suitable;

(*c*) while-you-wait information systems and remote computing facilities resemble reservation systems in requiring a quick initial response, but their users are then content to wait for 10 to 20 seconds for results; indeed they may be upset by too rapid a response, for this suggests that their request was a trivial one, or that it may have been misunderstood as such.

When designing a real-time system there is a standing temptation to provide a very rapid response because it is technically possible and more exciting to do so; but there can be a very rapid rise in cost as the response time is reduced, for it depends on the peak rather than the mean load capacity of the computer. Those items that provide a rapid response time are expensive; in particular, data storage units are needed that can hold very large commercial files and give rapid access to any item in the file. The only units currently available are magnetic discs and drums, which because they are slow have to be backed by magnetic core or integrated circuit storage of much smaller capacity and higher cost; this combination is clumsy, costly, critical in its air-conditioning requirements, prone to internal congestion, and wasteful of computer time, which it uses to shuffle its data about among its various levels. As a result, real-time systems have occasionally achieved quite spectacularly low efficiencies, some having devoted less than 10 per cent of their time to useful work, while tying up the remainder in their own red tape. There is an urgent need for improved devices for storing large files of data; the problem has attracted a great deal of attention and the development of electronics will undoubtedly displace our great whirling discs and spinning drums into the museums of technology that they are destined—even designed, to encumber. The cost penalty of real-time operation will then fall considerably, and it may replace batch working for ordinary use. However, until we change our sleeping habits the real-time demand will continue to drop by night, at which time batch processing will be used to mop up after the day's real-time activities; that is, to weed ephemera and time-expired data from the files, and to produce operating statistics and charging information.

The intelligent terminals mentioned in the previous chapter provide the most common current example of a network of computers operating in real time over data links. They illustrate also what could become a very significant trend in the development of information engineering systems, namely, the dissemination of computing functions throughout the network, as opposed to their concentration in a few major centres. Many of the operations in computer networks are concerned with the routine management of communications and of data storage and retrieval, with data input and output, and these are tasks that can be delegated to small, satellite computers. Satellite machines could gradually take on more significant functions, for example they could carry out some of the preliminary stages of processing by rejecting the irrelevant, correcting errors and consolidating data from a group of terminals; they could provide an immediate 'tactical' response in a control system and report back in summary form to the central 'strategic' control computers. The example of animal nervous systems suggests that there may well be advantages in this line of approach, and also points to some risks, for when data have been pre-digested in this way some information has been lost, and an interpretation has been superimposed on the raw stuff; while this is helpful in the circumstances for which it was designed, it can mislead in others—just as pre-processing in the retina reduces the load on the optic nerve and on the brain, but can give rise to optical illusions.

When the production of large-scale integrated circuits has become flexibly automatic it will be possible to produce short runs of tailor-made micro-computers on single chips having built-in programs for special purpose functions, and to do so quickly and cheaply enough for them to be thrown away and replaced when the system grows or extends, or when its users' needs or circumstances alter. Information engineering design will then enter into a new phase of development and match our requirements to a degree unknown today. Today's systems are terse, unhelpful, and unforgiving: tomorrow's will be tolerant of the errors and ignorances of an amateur making one of his infrequent forays into computer territory. These amiable systems of the future will fully justify their extra cost for they will promote fruitful relationships with many who today are frightened or repelled by the mechanical difficulties of communicating with our cruder machines. Here lies a real need for fully interactive working, and so far real time.

Intelligent terminals also promise to alleviate one of the more severe practical difficulties that plague the construction of large information engineering systems, and that are inherent in the very rapid obsoloescence of electronic equipment. The time-scale of this obsolescence has now fallen below the time needed to implement a major system; 'if it works, it's obsolete' is no longer a cynical quip, it is an unpalatable truth: and it is one that is becoming more troublesome as systems become larger and more complex, and as they cross international boundaries. Different components are installed at different times and have different rates of obsolescence, and to require that each be replaced by its exact equivalent would be to exclude the benefit of technological advance. It is essential to design the system in a loose-jointed way which allows its parts to be replaced without making it necessary to recast the whole. The straightforward approach is to define critical boundaries or 'interfaces' between components or subsystems, and to standardize the conditions to be met in exchanges of data and control signals and messages across them. Pre-programmed computers, cheap enough to be replaced when a component, a subsystem, or external circumstances change could be invaluable as mediators at these interfaces.

The change from batch to real-time processing is accompanied by substantial changes in the manning of the computer system itself. In a real-time system all files have to be ready for instant use, and the input and output traffic flows through telecommunication channels; hence, the operators who in batch working change magnetic tapes, tend punched-card readers and high-speed line-printers, and carry decks of cards and mountains of output stationery to and fro are not needed; nor are the hot, noisy, dusty, and oily machines which they serve. To a manager accustomed to the exciting hurly-burly of batch processing a real-time computer room can be an unnervingly empty and apparently idle place, nor is it easy for him to accept that no one knows exactly what the computer is doing at any moment. Again, real-time computer rooms are not surrounded by a sea of girls all punching cards, or by rooms filled with bursters, guillotines, envelopers, and all the other bustling impedimentia of batch working. But the manager's loss is the user's gain, for he now has direct contact with and control over the computer which does his work on demand, where previously he had to send it to some remote data laundry that washed it as it thought fit, and in its own time.

To recapitulate, the real meaning of real-time is operating in a time-scale that is relevant to the particular real-world circumstances and needs of a user. It involves on-line working, but 'on-line' has a wider denotation than 'real-time'. Interactive systems are both on-line and real-time, and often they are time-sharing as well; but 'time-sharing' has a wider range than this. Any of these methods of working may or may not use a telecommunications link. 'On-line' is a slippery term which has nothing to do with the use of a telecommunications line—but when such a line is used it usually works on-line to the computer, and so the brief form 'on-line' is widely used with a meaning that would be more strictly conveyed by 'remote on-line'.

Private roads or public highways ?

8

Some problems

The convergence of computing and telecommunications through digital technology and mutual need, and the emergence of information engineering systems combining both functions, raise numerous questions; but there is a prior question: do we need an explicit public policy for their joint development, or can we safely leave it to the interplay of economic forces? The broader social implications of information engineering are the subject of the next chapter, but it is evident enough that their potential importance for trade and industry, for governments and individuals, can hardly be overstated. The issues of commercial effectiveness, personal liberty, and state control are ones of substantial public concern, with strong political overtones which no government dare ignore. Unfortunately, they also involve matters of great technical complexity in which we have little or no relevant experience; however, they will not go away, and we must do the best we can.[6] [7]

We have to ask how information engineering systems should be provided and operated? Telecommunications service is provided by 'common carriers', which when they are not owned and operated by the state as monopolies are closely regulated by a government agency. What should be the carriers' role in systems using computers? Our initial essays in using computers remotely have employed the carriers' networks, for these were the most obvious instruments; and some computer men appear to have been surprised to find that these networks had been designed with telephones rather than data circuits in view! Data transmission has, therefore, developed principally as an extension of the carriers' existing monopoly services. Should this continue? Or, should the carriers compete freely with others? and do so for their public as well as for their private services? Should they even be excluded from what is certainly a new market sector, if not an entirely new service?

Again, in the information systems of the future as the computing function becomes dispersed, and as computer-like devices are used to switch messages and to process signals in telecommunication systems, will it be desirable or even possible to exclude the carriers from providing and operating computing services also? As Lawrence pointed out, we have a propensity for mistaking our maps for the real world, but as time passes the neat artifical boundaries which we draw for our administrative or academic convenience shift and blur, and I doubt whether the difference between computing and communication can be kept clear enough to permit the definition of an enduring and legally enforcable boundary. Would it, indeed, make economic sense to keep computing and communications apart? If not, then on what terms should the carriers participate in the market for computer services? Conversely, should those who provide distributed computing services be allowed to offer some forms of telecommunications service also?

Data transmission is different

Are the problems posed by data transmission really so different from those of telephony that they need separate treatment? Or, is it only that they are those of a more coherent, articulate, and technically-minded group of telecommunications customers—and one moreover which is backed by a 'rival' industry? Certainly, major differences do arise from the fact that data messages are sent and received by machines, whereas telecommunications have evolved to handle messages between men. Men are flexible and intelligent, tolerant of errors and differences in format, and communicate at low speeds using a limited variety of terminal instruments. Data terminals are of many varieties, and are produced by a wide range of competing manufacturers whose requirements for speed and for control signals differ, and for whom standardization is anathema. The devices to be linked, the courses, volumes, and incidences of their traffic streams, and the economic factors which apply, are all different for human and machine communications.

Again, the operational requirements for data transmission are less homogenous than those of telephony. First, a computer can emit data faster than most telecommunication channels can swallow it, can do so all day and all night, and the bulk transmission of this vast output is economically sensitive to channel bandwidth and cost. The second, and largest, group of users consists of those who interrogate remote information systems, and they are less affected by channel bandwidth than they are by channel switching time, for that directly affects the speed of response; these users find the several seconds required by today's telephone systems troublesomely long, and they are disturbed to know that it is likely to be reduced only slowly, as electronic circuits gradually displace the ponderous mechanical selectors of Strowger and crossbar exchanges. The third group of users, the occasional customers of shared computing services, are not very sensitive to channel switching time or to channel bandwidth, but they are extremely sensitive to cost.

Private roads or public highways?

Costs and charges

Computer men complain continually about the high costs of data
transmission, for they feel that the carriers' charges are set more by the
history and circumstances of the telephone system than by the market
value of the service given to them. Some of their plaint is no more than
the normal market chaffering; some arises because they have not properly evaluated the economics of remote real-time working in their
particular application; but some genuine points remain. First, the structure of the carriers tariff schedules does tend to derive from their main
business; thus, wide-band channels are relatively much cheaper than
the narrow ones—the charges increase as the square root of the bandwidth rather than proportionately. For instance, although a short local
48 kbits/second channel is expensive, links longer than about 70 km
cost only about as much as 3 or 4 speechband channels each capable of
2·4 kbits/second. Data customers would like to exploit this circumstance
by sharing one wideband channel between several of them, but the
carriers do not allow this; after all they are in the retail business themselves. They are also somewhat shocked at the impudence of a customer
who believes himself able to beat them at their own business of dividing
channels, and not least when he happens to be one who as yet brings
them very much less revenue than their traditional and less demanding
telephone customers.

Many data customers believe that they should pay only for the
amount of data conveyed (channel bandwidth X time) and not also for
the distance, on the ground that the benefit to them is largely independent of distance; and by analogy with the postal service in which also
the costs reside more in local collection and delivery than in long-distance
carriage. Certainly for some telecommunication facilities, for example a
satellite, the costs are not proportional to distance; and in some countries
satellites could come to be used for domestic as well as for international
transmission. Moreover, there is no reason to suppose that the allocation
of the carriers' overheads and other fixed costs is any less arbitrary than
it is in other businesses, and when such costs are high they dilute any
dependence of cost on distance. It would also be naïve to imagine that
prices bear a simple fixed arithmetical relationship to the corresponding
costs—even when these can be satisfactorily dissected out of the mass; in
all businesses, pricing is primarily a marketing matter. These points are
illustrated by comparing the charge for a speechband channel over the
public switched network with that for an equivalent leased private channel: for instance, for a 300-km link in Western Europe and North America
the amount of public call time which could be purchased by one month's
rental of the private channel ranged (in 1972) from 26 to 90 hours. There
is no harmonization of the tariff schedules of different countries, and
this adds difficulties and irritation into the economic design of international data systems.

The cost problem is compounded by the effects of rapid technical development in electronics. For a given level of performance the costs of computing equipment have been falling at about 50 per cent per annum, whereas the corresponding rate for telecommunications has been nearer 2 per cent. Were these trends to continue they would soon provide a powerful incentive to use intelligent terminals in order to reduce the bandwidth needed, and also to use local computers rather than remote services; both of these would curb the growth of demand for data transmission. The nature and extent of a user's need for data-transmission services goes with his acquisition of computing equipment, and his computer supplier has a considerable influence on the system he adopts; clearly, suppliers will tend to recommend the use of the intelligent terminals which they do supply rather than the data communications which they do not. The common carrier can be expected to do the opposite, and the interest of the individual user may fall between two stools. His interest also, may differ from the 'national interest', for it can be argued that this somewhat amorphous concept requires the widest possible diffusion of terminal services, and therefore the provision of cheap wideband links in order to allow the use of the simplest and cheapest terminals. If indeed wideband links came to be used nationally for the distribution of a more varied choice of domestic television programmes then they could be used also for information and computing services. However, in an alternative and equally plausible scenario a single-chip micro-computer is installed in every home for the local control of various domestic appliances, and for their remote interrogation and command, and this computer could serve also as an intelligent terminal, thus reducing the need for wideband transmission. These and many other technological possibilities make it extremely difficult to discern any pattern in the very fluid future of information engineering.

Telecommunications costs may not fall as rapidly as those of computing, but as they fall the users' emphasis will shift from cost to dependability; this indeed may arrest the decline in cost because of the need to duplicate some links in order to guard against channel failure, and also to exchange frequent routine messages over every link to reveal the onset of failure. Channel failure is not the only, nor the most troublesome, threat to the integrity of data networks: the loss, theft, or destruction of data; the unauthorized deletion of data or programs; their clandestine examination; the insertion of false material; hardware and software faults, and illicit modifications; the use of channels vulnerable to cross-talk, accidental crossed connections, or to interception by tapping or by picking up stray electromagnetic radiation; all of these present hazards that must be evaluated. The standard countermeasures include the use of passwords, physical control over access to terminals and to channel equipment, cryptographic techniques, restraints on the reading and writing of data files and programs and their periodic dumping onto magnetic tapes, and computer programs and procedures which log every use of the system and flag abnormal patterns of use. None of this can be done for nothing, and detailed studies are necessary to show what can be afforded in the light of the circumstances of each particular application. Different methods will be used in channel-switched and packet-switched systems. Protection against channel failure is always easier and more economic to provide in large networks, which for the small user argues for the use of the public switched network in which redundancy arises naturally from the overconnection needed to allow any pair of the entire population of terminals to be linked.

The use of data transmission

When we are considering whether data transmission really is different from telephony we do well to bear in mind that it serves several quite different purposes:

(*a*) dispersion, as in the collection of data from a number of remote locations—branches, shops, offices, and factories;

(*b*) diversity, as when a time-sharing bureau provides a variety of specialist services more effectively than its customers could do for themselves;

(*c*) integration, as when a large national organization (such as a bank) uses data transmission to co-ordinate its affairs;

(*d*) resource sharing, for example to provide back-up against overloads or breakdowns, or when a group of users share one large computer.

These different purposes have different patterns of demand. The collection of data may employ a polling system to collect several seconds' worth of data regularly from each of a number of fixed points in rotation, whereas in an airline's seat reservation system we have a fluctuating demand from a wide scatter of points with messages that may last from a few seconds to several minutes. Information and computing services also require access to a wide dispersion of points, and incur transmission times ranging from a few seconds to 30 minutes or more; their pattern of demand is far from fixed, for habits have not had time to set, moreover the development of cheap and powerful pocket calculators and their inevitable association with cassette tapes will capture some part of what might have provided a substantial demand for computer bureau services. Remote access to a bureau will, however, continue to offer up-to-date information services, and the data-transmission demand arising from bureau work may rest on information rather than on computation. Some have dreamed of a national computer 'grid', but in the electrical energy grid the economies of scale offered by central generation more than offset the diseconomies of distribution; applied to computing the analogy holds for current information services, but not for raw computing power—except in the rare cases which need time on the most powerful computer available, but massive calculations of that kind are not usually done at the drop of a hat.

The diversity of requirements for data transmission is bound to increase, for the number of users has so far been rather small, and mainly limited to large organizations. We may see a major expansion into the home, for the manufacturers of integrated circuits will not long forgo this most massive and least demanding of markets. Because data transmission is in its early days its users have no solid ground of experience on which to frame their present and future needs, or to assess their economics; and the carriers have no useful records of past demand to guide their forecasts. Market surveys have sought to determine future needs, for instance 'The Eurodata Study 1972' commissioned by the carriers of 17 European countries, but they are all bedevilled by the uncertainties of inexperience, for they can only rely on potential users guessing what and how much they think they might want, and by when. Nonetheless, it is important to do all that we can to quantify the requirement, for this period happens to be one in which many carriers face extremely rapid telephone growth combined with the conversion from mechanical to electronic methods of switching, and there is therefore an unprecedented competition for the very large capital sums required.

Data transmission and the common carriers

Data transmission may be a different animal from telephony, but the carriers quite reasonably ask why it should not continue to employ their existing networks and expertise? They have the advantage of national coverages, and should be well placed to win all the advantages of scale—although these arise more in long-distance transmission than in the much larger investment in local distribution. The unique advantage possessed by the telephone authorities is, indeed, the extremely wide spread of outlets which they can offer to data terminals that are capable of being coupled to any telephone. The carriers have every reason to fear an erosion of their traditional business, for if it were decided to allow private companies to carry data, what logic would prevent their eventual operation as general carriers also?

However, the users and suppliers of computing equipment are ready to cite various objections to extending the carriers' monopolies to cover data services also, thus:

(*a*) the need for costly modems to adapt digital data to a network designed to carry analogue signals;

(*b*) high error rates caused by switching disturbances and noise insufficient to trouble the telephone user, but which have to be countered with cumbersome and expensive equipment and procedures;

(*c*) generally low maximum speed, and an inadequate choice of speeds;

(*d*) saturation of the network in the telephone busy periods (9–12 hours, 14–16 hours);

(*e*) transmission quality variable between different routes, and between successively dialled calls between the same parties;

(*f*) too much time lost due to faults;

(*g*) divided responsibility for service, leading to confusion and argument in the attribution of errors to channel or computer failures.

The carriers have also been criticized for being too rigid in their connection requirements, although many of them have now limited themselves to the minimum needed for electrical safety and to prevent mutual interference between users and with the signals used in the control of telephone switching. Safety requires protective connecting arrangements, including mains isolating transformers, high-voltage limiters, and fuses. Control of interference requires restraint on the frequencies used, on the maximum signal power, and on the distribution of energy within the signal spectrum and outside it. Inevitably, this brings up the supply of modems. Telephone systems contain a heterogenous mixture of channels and equipment provided over several decades, and changing continually as obsolete equipment is renewed, and to meet new patterns of traffic and demands for growth. The carrier is responsible for maintaining the quality of the telephone service, and also for adhering to international standards, and in my view he must retain control over the design and method of use of data modems associated with the public switched network. The easiest course is for the carrier to provide and maintain these modems, and many customers will be content that he should do so; but I believe that he should also encourage innovation by issuing specifications and approving proposals for modems to be supplied and maintained by others. These others, however, must for their part accept that occasional changes will be necessary in the interests of the telephone service—for the tail must go where the dog is going. Over leased private channels users can clearly be permitted to use any modem they choose, subject only to the fewest possible regulations directed at safety and interference.

Some of the complaints made by data customers have undoubtedly arisen because they have come up against large well-established organizations with strongly developed ideas and patterns of behaviour, which can make the carriers seem unresponsive to the needs of data when these differ from those of the familiar telephone user. Nor is there always an easy or effective way for an individual to bring his complaints home to a monopoly supplier who regards his main business as lying elsewhere. The carriers have not been accustomed to produce to outsiders the detailed technical and commercial information which data system designers need for planning; in particular, individual contract pricing rather than a published schedule of tariffs has been a frequent cause of complaint. Again, data transmission seems to be set for explosive growth, and doubts have been voiced about the ability and the readiness of the carriers to cope with it at the same time as they face a surge in demand for telephones. As public monopolies the carriers are restricted by their governments to very modest rates of return on their capital investments and, as they have also been accustomed to equipment that had much longer economic lives than computers, this tends to make them sceptical of data projects, for they see these as high-risk investments that are denied an appropriately high rate of return. They are, moreover, judged by the success of the telephone service, for neither the public nor their governments have much awareness of how important it is not to fail to provide a satisfactory data service also. The prospective data customer suspects, therefore, that in the internal competition for limited resources and for money the issue may not be decided in his favour. Some telephone authorities have indeed been inclined to play down the future needs of data, arguing that at least 90 per cent of the need will be met by channels of 2400 bits/second capacity or less, and 99 per cent by 10 000 bits/second. If single-chip computers take over most of the routine aspects of computing they may well be correct in these estimates, but I believe that after a brief respite much more complicated applications will develop and the demand will rise for channels of the widest bandwidths that the current technology can provide at reasonable cost. The carriers have no option but to take data transmission very seriously: if they do not they risk a most severe erosion of their future business as many of the now profitable commercial uses of the telephone are replaced by data messages between computers. Discussion and liason between organizations engaged in computing and in telecommunications is not helped by their different business styles: one is competitive and brash, the other is monopolistic and conservative; one enjoys the freedom of a private company, the other bears the weight of public and national responsibility; one can raise its risk capital on the money markets, the other has often been used by the government as an instrument of economic management.

Alternatives to the carriers

These various objections have led computer specialists to argue for the establishment of a data network separate from the telephone system; but it has not always been clear whether they wanted separate ownership, or totally separate equipment, or merely separate switching. Separate ownership would not necessarily reduce prices, for the business of providing a large national network can never be a free market—the entry costs are prohibitive. In most countries, indeed, only the state would be capable of supporting so large a project. Nor would it necessarily mean greater freedom of design, for it is unlikely that any data network could escape all government regulation, and the advantages and conveniences of standardization and integration would soon emerge, and these are

71

words which imply a substantial measure of monopoly. The existence of
a monopoly, whether public (de jure) or private (de facto), raises a number
of policy questions of great concern to data system users. Thus, what
terms should apply to service agreements? Are controls necessary to
ensure fair treatment between competing users? What criteria should
determine the location, amount, and timing of additions to the network?
How, indeed, can users be assured that suitable channels will be made
available at times and places to match their plans? Can the quality of
service be guaranteed in terms of response time, errors, interruptions,
and so on? The mere listing of these points indicates that data transmission customers are likely to seek much more detailed and explicit
assurances than the carriers have been accustomed to offer to their
telephone customers: nor is this mere peevishness; data transmission is
necessarily very closely coupled to the efficient design and effective
performance of the information engineering systems of which it is so
vital a part.

In the U.S.A., as a result of a judgement by the Federal Communications Commission, there has appeared a new kind of enterprise—the
specialized common carrier. These can offer data services at cheaper
rates than the general carriers, in part because they can achieve economies
of specialization (for their networks do not have to cope with telephony
also). But, in part they achieve economies because they are not required
to cover all parts of the country, serving the empty rural areas as well as
the crowded cities. This situation offers opportunities for what the general
carriers stigmatize as 'cream skimming', and it could conflict with national
policies for regional development. Again, because the plant of the specialized carriers is all new it will at this stage be more cost-effective than the
older parts of the general carriers' plant. Here we see revealed one of the
problems that plague the setting of charges; should a customer pay only
for those items of plant that he actually uses? Or should his charge be
averaged over the whole system—or all plant of the same kind?

One alternative to a completely private data system would be for the
common carriers to provide the channels, and for the switching to be
left either to the customers themselves or to separate companies. Such
bodies as the banks and the airlines already employ private networks
provided over channels leased from the carriers, and there are examples
also of private networks operated by a consortium of users in the same
line of business. Networks of these types could be opened up to general
use: the arguments for and against doing so resemble those that apply to
the specialized common carriers, although the use of the centrally planned national telecommunications network offers to produce a more
homogeneous and systematic development, rather than one at the mercy
of sectional or local pressures--but this last argument can be reversed to
form the complaint of insensitivity to the customer's needs. In my view,

it would not be sensible to duplicate the huge investments which the common carriers have made in national networks, not least because developments in electronics will allow the traffic capacity of these existing networks to be greatly increased; nor should we fail to conserve scarce natural resources, whether these be hills for microwave relay stations, geostationary orbits for satellites, or channels in the radio-frequency spectrum. I favour exploiting the carriers' networks rather than attempting to build anew for digital data. Nor do I think that data channels should be segregated within a carrier's system, for I believe that all telecommunication services will adopt digital methods as opportunity permits, thus producing an eventual integration that will bring economies in design, installation, maintenance, training, and in the provision of reserves to cover breakdowns and growth. Because in their own interests carriers have no option but to take data seriously, I would like them to be the agents who provide national systems of 'dataways' which would operate as motorways rather than as railways; that is, subject to the fewest possible traffic and safety rules and on payment of standard tolls, they would be open for all to use as they pleased, and not be restricted to the company's vehicles and drivers only.

It does seem to me, however, that we shall need separate switching equipment for data signals at least until most telephone signals are digital, that is for some years yet, for data traffic is an uncomfortably spiky bedfellow for speech; moreover, the traffic patterns and customer behaviours are very different. No one has anywhere near enough experience to rule on the relative merits of channel and packet switching. Packet switching offers no panacea; and channel switching, speeded up and made less noisy and more reliable by electronics, will prove its worth in private networks, and perhaps also in the handling of long messages in public switched networks. The buffering and processing capabilities of packet switching seem to me to suit it best to a public network designed to convey short messages between the widest possible range and variety of users, computers, and terminals. My own inclination is not to distinguish between channel and packet switching, but between public and private use; and I assume that users will be free to switch their private networks in any way they please. The cream-skimming argument persuades me against private competion for public systems; although this argument would become less compelling if the government were prepared to recompense the common carrier for uneconomic services provided to meet social needs or in response to its regional development policies. However, this possibility raises a very much bigger question which has repercussions into the telephone and telegraph services—and, indeed, beyond telecommunications altogether. In the present, early stage of packet switching there could be merit in competitive innovation, and my inclination would be to license private companies to operate packet switching systems over channels leased from the carriers, and by a kind of reverse cream-skimming to apply the license fees plus a royalty on their turnover to compensate the carrier for plugging the uncommercial gaps left by the companies with his own packet-switching services. And, until the results of competition in packet switching became clear I believe that channel switching for public use is best left with the carriers.

Standards

In any public or multi-user network standard connection requirements are necessary to avoid mutual interference and to ensure adequate service. There is a natural human tendency, exaggerated by large organizations, to specify more than is strictly necessary, but to avoid cramping future designers the standards set should be as few and as far-sighted as possible. Standards may, for instance, be needed for:

(*a*) speeds—preferred values will ensure that the operating speeds of different users terminals are compatible, although differing speeds can be accommodated by providing sufficient buffer storage;

(*b*) codes—ideally the network should be code-transparent, but because the message must be intelligible to the receiver there will need to be a preliminary 'handshaking' exchange of messages in a standard control language and procedure to confirm compatibility before transmission beings;

(*c*) format—ideally the network should impose no restrictions, but here also the receiver may need to be sent a standard preliminary signal to indicate what format is being used by the sender;

(*d*) transmission control procedures for setting-up and clearing down calls;

(*e*) electrical inferface, specifying connections and signal characteristics;

(*f*) principles and techniques for charging for the use of the system.

It is the habit of standards to arrive too late, for they have powerful adversaries who delay them on the way. Suppliers, installation managers, and users of computers all have masses of existing idiosyncractic practices, files, and equipment which they are naturally most anxious to protect— even from improvement—and computer programmers and systems designers demand total creative freedom, and abhor all restraint. Equipment salesmen thrive on exciting differences and oppose unexploitable uniformity. The difficulties of standardization, and particularly of international standardization, are tremendous, but I retain some hope that the use of stored-program processors produced cheaply and reliably on a single integrated-circuit chip will supply the means to marry up diverse systems and thus greatly reduce the need for standards.

Data processing and the carriers

The policy questions raised are not confined to data transmission. Are the ancillary processes associated with data networks—for example, error control, code conversion, polling, concentration, and the intermediate storage of messages with or without editing, to be regarded as communication or as processing? Should the common carriers perform such processes? Or, should they be restricted to a completely transparent role in which they simply accept a stream of bits for delivery without change? Throughout the networks of the future we are certain to see a much wider diffusion of computing power as minicomputers become low enough in price and high enough in reliability to be fitted and forgotten. This distributed 'intelligence' within the network could have very significant consequences for design, and for demand; and it deserves the earliest evaluation. Again, what is to be the role of the carriers in data processing proper? Should they be excluded althogether? Or be allowed to compete 'on equal terms' (whatever that may mean)? Or be given a monopoly of computing services? Few would argue for this last, but in its favour it is worth recalling that government regulation of the carriers obliges them to serve any member of the public at reasonable rates, and on a regular and equitable basis. If the carriers were to be allowed to compete with others then they must do so fairly: for instance, they should neither deny data-transmission services to their rivals, nor provide them on any less favourable basis than to themselves. Some have concluded from this that a carrier operating a data-processing service should do so as a separate subsidiary company, and perhaps as one which is forbidden to serve its parent. This last restraint is too severe; it is principally directed at competitive pricing deriving 'unfairly' from economies of scale, but that is an argument which equally well applies to the computing services offered by any other large organization, such as a bank, an airline, or a computer manufacturer. In my view, the carriers should be treated no differently from any other organization whose business is not primarily the operation of a computing service. Indeed, there is merit in allowing them to obtain first-hand experience of the problems faced by their data customers.

Those who would close the computing services market to the carriers often represent that they would use the profits of the telephone business to undercut their competitors. Cross-subsidies are not entirely unknown in PTT's, for the telephone service has occasionally been used to support an ailing postal service; but it is always open to a much greater degree of government supervision and control than are the internal accounting arrangements of private companies. A more plausible line of argument is that the carriers might not match the fast pace of innovation as well as would a computer entrepreneur, and would thus deny their customers the reduced costs that arise from technical advance: but this is an argument against a carriers' monopoly of computing, not against their presence in a competitive market. The carriers do have their hands very full with their traditional business, and telephone users are most vocal in arguing that nothing should be allowed to distract their attention from that.

It is worth spending a moment on the suggestions for a national computer network. The case is made that about one-half of the installed computer capacity is unused and could be made available at very cheap rates given an economical data-transmission network. This may be doubted for at least two reasons. First, the times when computers are not being used are the 'anti-social' night hours, and at weekends; second, bitter experience of attempting to make arrangements for mutual support shows how rare it is for two apparently identical computer installations to be alike enough to permit even the planned exchange of work, and the scope for the casual use of idle capacity seems likely to be limited. Spare capacity is one side of a coin, the other side of which is the dumping of excess capacity to the detriment of orderly growth. Dumping could have its traditional international connotation if one country's surplus were to be sold below cost to its neighbours over international data links; and some have foreseen computing loads chasing the sun through the time zones. If, however, a significant proportion of a country's computing capacity were to be provided by a national or international computer grid it would become vulnerable to industrial action by a very small number of militants, and would inevitably become an attractive target for it on both economic and political grounds. The case for doing computing remotely is probably an ephemeral one, which rests on the current costs of computing and communications; but the case for providing nation-wide access to up-to-date sources of data will endure: data transmission, therefore, may be much more employed in the carriers' traditional business of conveying information than in the distribution of raw computing power.

If the carriers are not excluded from providing computing services, should the purveyors of computing services be excluded from offering telecommunication services to their customers over channels which they have leased in bulk from the carriers? The carriers customary monopoly covers all A-to-B communications where A and B are members of different organizations, or different private persons; but when A and B are customers of the same on-line computer bureau how can they be prevented from exchanging messages? They can quite legitimately share a data file, and when A writes an item into the file and B subsequently reads it have they been guilty of communication? How does this differ from packet switching, which also involves storage and delay? Do the carriers' monopolies cover delayed communications of this kind, in which a shared computer file is used to provide an electronic letter-drop service?

The policy problems are quite tangled enough on a national scale, but they have international complications also, some of which arise from the operations of multi-national companies. Certain computer bureaux offer information and computing services from computers located in other countries. What are the implications for foreign affairs, commercial and political, of the storage of important information in the data bank of a foreign country, and of that country's access to ours? Shall we see the data equivalents of numbered Swiss accounts, flags of convenience, and Mexican divorces? What might this mean for legislation which required disclosure, for commercial or legal reasons, for taxation, or to protect the privacy of an individual? Shall we need extradition treaties for data as well as for people?

Again, the evident dominance of American firms in the supply of computer hardware has implications for national sovereignty. Thus, is it acceptable for so important a component of one country's infrastructure to remain at the mercy of the national policies of another—or even of company policies decided by private individuals seeking purely commercial optimizations? What should be the role of multi-national corporations in international policy-making? Some of them are larger economic entities than many states, and exercise as much influence on the substance of policy formation as these states do on its shadow. Should we be more energetic in pursuing international standards for computing? Telecommunications enjoys long-established standards, but it has also had a low rate of innovation which has prevented its costs from dropping as rapidly as they might have done: computing has next to no standards, and none of any long term significance, but its costs have fallen dramatically, and still dip sharply downwards. One international matter of great concern is the communication satellite; in the West these have been operated by an international consortium acting as the "carriers' carrier", but geostationary orbits are a limited natural resource and their allocation can be expected to cause increasing political difficulty in the future.

For national policy, the choice is broadly between a centrally planned development of data services and their unco-ordinated growth by accretion. The parties concerned are the public, the users of computing and data services, the suppliers of these services and of their equipment, the common carriers, and the government. The public and the users are heterogenous collections with no group identity or corporate representation. The suppliers and the carriers are strong pressure groups, with clear commercial interests, and they know their way blindfold through the corridors of power. The government has diverse interests. It either operates or regulates the common carriers, and it determines their investment policy. It is itself a very large computer user, and it seeks to promote the prosperity of its native industry—including its information engineering industry. It is responsible also for protecting the public against invasion of their privacy and other abuses arising from the concentration of power which a high-centralized computer network may foster. The government's duty is to look after 'the national interest', although when he hears that phrase the taxpayer does well to think in terms of subsidies. With so many diverse interests and parties, how can we best decide what policy to follow? And which should be the executive arm that ensures that it is quickly and properly made effective? The two main constituent industries remain separate, and each appears to be content to harvest the crop that lies immediately before it. Of course, industries are figments of the economists' imaginations, for only firms exist; and some firms cover both constituents, but they reveal little evidence of internal communication. In the meantime, private data networks proliferate and there is an uneasy feeling abroad that we may be missing a unique opportunity to navigate rather than drift.

How important is it that data communication and computing services should be adequate and timely? Is it important enough to divert resources from other pressing matters? The advocates of action see enormous benefits coming—but not just yet. Computing and data communications are like vitamins; when times are hard it is easy to give them up and no immediate trouble ensues, but in the long term the constitution is weakened and the future prejudiced beyond the point of recovery. Japan has decided to take the prospects very seriously, and has a national programme for the development of information technology. Canada, also, has examined the provision of trans-continental data link as a major national effort. Any country that hopes for a major share of the world's trade in the manufacture and export of information engineering systems must be able to point to experience of successful operation at home if it is to carry conviction among customers abroad. I am persuaded that the development of information engineering is of such potential significance that it should be the subject of explicit study and report, for it is of key importance to suppliers, carriers, and users alike that the right products, services, and expertise should become available at the right time. There is nowhere near enough communication between the parties at present. In particular, I believe that the effects of using single-chip computers as expendable components, and distributing them freely as donkey engines throughout information engineering systems, needs to be properly evaluated. Their influence on design and on demand could be profound, and their potential for processing the data collected without the users' knowledge, and thus affecting the results produced, may also be of great significance.

9

Total information and the whole man

This chapter will not rehash the commonplace of the cashless society, or proclaim the horrors of the data bank. Nor will it present a coherent scenario of life in a total information society, for that has been persuasively and wittily done by Johanneson.[8] It will simply look at some of the social issues and the policy questions that they pose.

It is an entirely reasonable lay reaction to enquire testily whether those in the information business are not taking themselves altogether too seriously. Are they behaving like Fat Boys trying to make our flesh creep? After all, men have been collecting, storing, processing, and exchanging information for a very long time: have today's experts just discovered this fact, as M. Jourdain discovered prose? Our answers will depend on how we appraise the changes in scale brought about by electronics. Over the last century the maximum rate at which information can be sent through an electrical channel has increased more than 100 million times, and an intricate web of channels has encircled and shrunk the world until a McLuhan can speak of a global village. Developments in other technologies have increased the pace and complexity of research, manufacturing, transport, and trade, all of which are now generating information at too fast a rate, with too high a precision, and in too great a volume for us to assimilate unaided; and we have not been allowed the time to adjust our ways to those of the machines we have begun to use to help us.

Human affairs have always been strongly affected by the current information technology. The invention of writing freed our forebears from the spatial restraints of face-to-face speech, and the temporal limitations of unaided memory. Within the span of history the speed and range of couriers set limits to the growth of empires: today, a government could cover at least our planet and its neighbours. Our institutions and our societies have evolved for survival in a pre-electronic environment, but today's torrent of instant information may dissolve and wash away their foundations. Up to now we have had to simplify ruthlessly and analyse crudely in order to manage the complexity of real life, but computers are giving us the capacity to deal with intricate systems as they are—or, at least, as we think they are. Powerful analytical skills are available as clip-on programs, packaged for instant use without the labour of learning, but also without submitting to the discipline of understanding their relevance, and their limitations.

Automation in industry, transport, and commerce is increasingly freeing us from routine matters and allowing us to concentrate on the setting of priorities and the choice of goals. We are entering also, into the latter stages of that shift from agriculture to manufacture to the service trades which marks a nation's economic evolution. In countries where this process is most advanced the service industries already occupy more than one-half of the working population, and the proportion is increasing. Information engineering will automate this sector also, and thus exert a considerable influence on national productivity. If productivity is one side of a coin, then unemployment is the other; and to be socially acceptable it must be shared out in the form of increased leisure. Mass education has so far paid little attention to the prospect of extended leisure, but salesmen know a vacuum when they see one, and the automated production of integrated circuits demands a large and expanding market. A leisure products industry will open up the mass domestic market. Its obvious strategy is to exploit the bridgehead established by television: if , by definition, one television programme is good, then two will be better; if two, then four . . . But, too few radio channels exist for direct broadcasting, and distribution cables and video-tape recorders will be used to feed existing television sets. Home cine also, will be recorded on magnetic-tape cassettes for instant replay on the television screen, and we shall see the development of a major new market in elaborate, but inexpensive, home apparatus for automatically recording pre-selected programmes—including those distributed on demand over the cables by night for screening the next day. Tape cassettes will thus become available for education along the lines of the Open University in Britain. This might begin stealthily through courses directed at sports, hobbies, and foreign travel, and be extended discreetly to cover the perennial re-training that the increasing pace of technological change will require. The scope for political influence through such a medium needs no emphasis.

The combination of television cable and screen requires the addition only of a simple keyboard, such as a push-button telephone, to become a terminal giving access to remote computing and information services. The drive to exploit the enormous capital investments in existing local telephone networks, and the pressure to sell electronics, will lead to the incorporation of a single-chip computer in these terminals; it will probably be pre-programmed in order to avoid troubles from unskilled programming—and to create a useful replacement market! This computer could provide for the local control of cookers, washing machines, central heating, television programme recording, burglar alarms, and telephone answering; and also for their remote command and interrogation by the household and by other authorized users, such as the meter-reading computers of the public utlities.[9] Pre-programmed chips could prove to be inconspicuous but most potent life changers, for very few people indeed would be able to understand in detail what they were doing, or even be aware that they were doing anything of real consequence. We will need to regulate and watch very closely those who choose and those who write the programs, for the opportunities for theft and fraud, and for manipulating our opinions and our purchasing habits, are rich indeed. As well as supporting our other leisure pursuits, information engineering will provide its own, for our domestic computers could be programmed to play chess and other war games, to occupy us with puzzles and quizzes, and to link us into the national Bingo game. They could even use audio-visual stimuli controlled by alpha-rhythm feedback to take us on programmed 'trips'; and the fatal fascination exercised by one-armed bandits suggests that machines are unlikely to be less addictive than the drugs which they replace—and certainly they would not long remain untaxed.

Our steadily growing use of computers in commerce and government is producing a more explicit rationality in our affairs, and an increased reliance on quantitative assessments. Economic modelling provides an example of this development, and a warning. We could accept its results too readily, believing that eminent economists and precise and expensive computers would not be used unless the data were accurate, the methods adequate, and the results relevant. We may be tempted to assume that complexity in the model implies clarity in the thinking. But, as we all know when the spell wears off, economic data are far from accurate or complete, and economic analysis presents a point of view rather than an objective account of reality. What we want is not bigger computers but better economists; a gram of insight, not a tonne of processing. Misplaced faith is not the only risk we run; alienation is another. Many public issues are too complex for laymen to understand, whether they be elected members of government or their electors. The use of computer modelling will raise our incomprehension to new heights, and reinforce our feeling that we cannot participate effectively in the democratic process. Government by experts is fine when it remains beneficient and escapes the pitfalls of sub-optimization—but neither proviso is likely to hold good. When to industrial and commercial automation we add the automation of government, men and women will fall outside the control loops, and we could become redundant ciphers in cyberland.[8] In a complex society government planning cannot avoid being complex and subtle, or affecting people who are unaware of its effects, or unable to counteract them. A split could open between the few who know and the many who do not, between the information-rich and the information-poor; a similar split could enlarge the gap between the economically advanced and the developing countries; hence the social effects of increased information could be divisive.[10]

A pincers attack is being mounted on the ordinary man as one jaw approaches him from industry, treating him as a consumer to be billed, invoiced, and analysed, and the other jaw approaches him from government treating him as a payer of taxes and receiver of pensions and social services. However, the ordinary man may also present his government with an interesting problem as he becomes a regular user of information engineering systems: thus, already city dwellers have more in common with each other, irrespective of the country they happen to live in, than they do with rural dwellers of their own countries. Similar communities of interest will tend to develop between scientists, engineers, bird-watchers, conservationists, chess players, and so on, and because each of us plays many different roles we could see the build-up of a complex pattern of multiple cross-linkages that transcend frontiers and take no account of party political boundaires.

None of these things will happen overnight; there is no call to battle stations, no reason for a Luddite revolt. The biggest current problem is to establish that there is a problem,[11] to convince governments that there are some real issues of policy and not just the anguished bleatings of a few experts out to bolster their own importance, or scared by their own cleverness. It is necessary also to demonstrate that the problems raised by information engineering are ones for us, and not for posterity; for although the latter may well be the more important they are unlikely to command the attention of those whose horizons are bounded by the next election, nor are they simple or clear enough to be used to much political effect. The immediate task is to identify the problem areas, to determine which interests can contribute, and which will want to; and to ascertain who will sponsor the necessary studies and pay for them. The government must be involved, so must the common carriers, the computer hardware and software suppliers, the users and suppliers of computer services, together with legal—and other more vivid—guardians of our civil liberties. If we turn away, and decide not to decide—or not yet—then an irresistible industrial momentum will sweep us ever 'forward' at speeds and to destinations which we have not chosen and may not like. This is no doomsday cry: it is a plea for awareness and conscious choice. Unless we decide to abdicate, or do so by neglect, we *can* control our machines before they control us—and make certain that Erewhon is nowhere.[12]

Appendix: Notes on Chapter 3

1. Baseband signals

The spectrum of an on/off binary pulse is sketched in Fig. 6(a) which indicates that the energy falls as the frequency rises, and that it drops to zero at frequencies related to the pulse duration; for example, the spectrum of a 1 millisecond pulse has zeros at $(1/0\cdot001) = 1000$ Hz, and at its harmonics 2000 Hz, 3000 Hz, and so on. In practical systems bandwidth is expensive, although with advances in electronics it is becoming less so, and it is neither practicable nor economic to attempt to preserve a perfect rectangular pulse shape by transmitting the entire spectrum. Moreover, it is useful to limit the frequency band accepted by the receiver in order to reject unwanted signals and noise outside the range containing the main signal energy. More than 80 per cent of the energy of a rectangular pulse is concentrated in the band below the first zero point $f = 1/t$ Hz, where t is the pulse duration in seconds, and Fig. 6(b) indicates the effect of cutting off the spectrum at that point. The result is to blur the sharp edges of the pulse, but not to a degree that causes difficulty in detecting its arrival at the receiver. The effects of restricting the signal bandwidth even more is illustrated in Figs 6(c) to 6(f) which show what happens to two adjacent pulses. When the bandwidth falls below $0\cdot5f$ the pulses run together and cannot reliably be distinguished. Clearly, the narrower (briefer) the pulse the wider is the bandwidth required to transmit it satisfactorily. Fig. 2 (Chapter 3) shows that RTZ working produces narrower pulses than does NRZ, and this in practice means that RTZ tends to be used only for short local links where bandwidth is cheap.

2. Bits and bauds

The use of 2^n signalling levels allows 2^n bits/second to be transmitted through each 1 Hz of a channel's bandwidth. Hence in a 2^n-level system a signalling speed of 1 Baud corresponds to a data rate of n bits/second.

Appendix

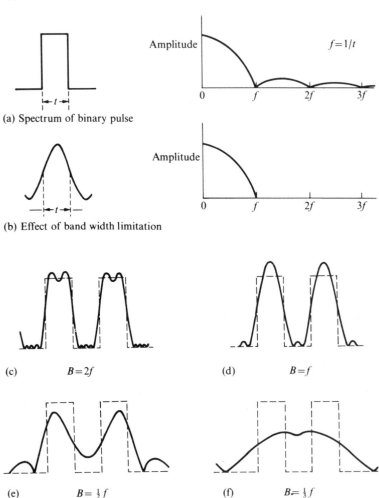

(a) Spectrum of binary pulse

(b) Effect of band width limitation

(c) $B = 2f$

(d) $B = f$

(e) $B = \frac{1}{2}f$

(f) $B = \frac{1}{3}f$

FIG. 6. Spectra and bandwidth.

3. Amplitude modulation

In amplitude modulation (AM) the data vary the amplitude of a higher frequency signal—the carrier wave—instead of varying the amplitude of a continuous electrical current. The effect of amplitude modulating a spectrum-limited pulse onto a carrier wave of frequency F Hz is shown in Fig. 7(a). The original signal baseband extended up to f Hz, and AM translates it to a frequency band of double this width situated equally above and below the carrier frequency. The part between F and $(F - f)$ is known as the 'lower sideband', and the part between F and

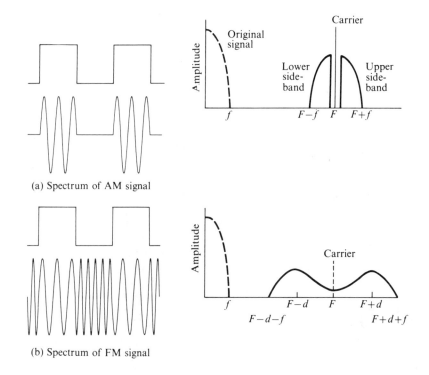

(a) Spectrum of AM signal

(b) Spectrum of FM signal

FIG. 7. Modulated waves

$(F + f)$ is the 'upper sideband'. When the baseband signal does not
extend down to zero frequency (that is, does not include a direct-
current component) it is not necessary to transmit both sidebands and
the bandwidth occupied by the modulated signal can be halved by suppressing either the upper or the lower sideband. Single-sideband working
(SSB) however, requires additional equipment at both sender and receiver
and its extra cost cannot usually be justified when the distance is short.
As Fig. 7(a) also suggests, a large proportion of the signal energy is concentrated in the carrier wave itself, and thus conveys no information. By
suppressing the carrier as well as one sideband the power-handling capability required by the sender, receiver, and channel amplifiers can be
considerably reduced, or alternatively for the same power specification
the useful signal components can be increased in strength. This benefit
is not gained without cost, for the carrier suppressed at the sending end
has to be reproduced exactly in the receiver in order to return the signal
to its baseband, and this can raise some quite difficult synchronization

problems. A compromise solution is not to eliminate the carrier wave and one sideband but to attenuate them, and this technique of 'vestigial sideband (VSB)' working is used in data links of medium length and it permits the transmission of a direct current component. This component can also be transmitted, and some power saved by transmitting both sidebands but suppressing the carrier; at the receiver a synchronized local carrier is reintroduced in a process called 'synchronous' or 'homodyne' detection.

4. Frequency modulation

In frequency modulation (FM) the data causes the frequency F Hz of the carrier to deviate from $(F - d)$ Hz for 0 to $(F + d)$ Hz for 1. As for AM, FM translates the data signal spectrum from its baseband to a range symmetrically disposed on either side of the carrier frequency. In FM, however, the energy distribution is more dispersed, to an extent determined by the deviation, d Hz, of the carrier frequency, as shown in Fig. 7(b). For a deviation of $\pm d$ Hz the bulk of the energy lies between $F - (d + f)$ and $F + (d + f)$, where f is the top frequency in the baseband. When the data rate is small compared with the deviation (that is, when f is smaller than d), the spectrum of the FM signal resembles that of two AM signals with carrier frequencies $(F - d)$ and $(F + d)$. A greater channel bandwidth is clearly required for FM than for AM, but the FM signal has the merit that it does not require carrier synchronization. Also, because the transmitted energy remains constant the signal can be limited to a fixed amplitude which makes the receiver less susceptible to disturbance by electrical noise, and so allows the use of less signalling power. We have here an example of a design trade-off of channel bandwidth against signal power, and the optimum solution will depend on the particular circumstances of the application and the current state of technology, for the relative costs of bandwidth and power will differ according to the length and location of the link, and will change as developments take place in cables, radio aerials, wave filters, digital processing equipment, and so on.

5. Phase modulation

The phase of a wave specifies the timing of the start of each of its cycles, and in phase modulation the data signal is caused to vary this timing for a carrier wave of constant amplitude. This usage of the term 'phase modulation' should not be confused with its use to describe a method of translating code groups into binary signals (see Fig. 3); the context will usually indicate which reference is intended. It can be shown by analysis that phase modulation of a carrier wave is equivalent to its frequency modulation by a baseband signal which has had the amplitudes of its higher frequency components increased in proportion to their frequencies. For binary data signals phase-reversal (180°) modulation is most often used, and is illustrated in Fig. 8(a). It is not possible to vary the phase of the carrier wave abruptly by more than ± 180°, for phase shifts of + 180° and −180° are indistinguishable, and so an n-level signal is usually transmitted by modulating the carrier phase in steps of ± 180°/n. Two binary data signals combined can produce four possible 'dibit' conditions (00, 01, 10, 11) and two such signals, or a single quaternary signal, are sometimes transmitted by the modulation of the carriers' phase to the four conditions −180°, −90°, +90°, +180° as shown in Fig. 8(b); this is known as quadrature modulation.

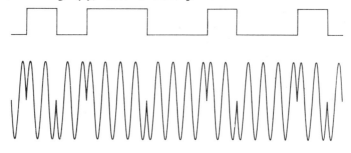

(a) Phase modulation (180°)

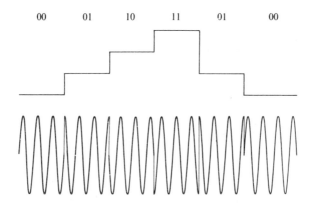

(b) Quadrature modulation

FIG. 8. Phase-modulated waves.

6. Synchronous modulation

Synchronous and asynchronous operation are discussed in Chapter 2 in terms of the data signalling rate. There is another sense in which these terms are used which refers to the relation between the signalling rate and the individual cycles of a carrier wave. When the carrier has a frequency that is an integral multiple of the data rate then in the 'on' states of an amplitude-modulated data signal an exact number of cycles of carrier oscillation will correspond to each bit, and the carrier frequency and data rate can then be synchronized. It is of particular advantage to do this when a low-frequency carrier is being used and the number of carrier wave cycles in each bit period is small, for then the number of carrier cycles is the same for each bit, which reduces fluctuations in the timing of the leading edges of each transition. This is the situation when frequency division multiplexing is employed over short-distance cable links for which it is not economic to use amplifiers to extend the frequency range transmitted, and for which therefore the carrier frequencies must be rather low. For long distance cables and for radio transmission the carrier frequencies are very high compared with the data rate and casual variations in the number of carrier cycles used to convey each bit produces an entirely insignificant amount of timing jitter. Synchronous modulation is worth while for phase modulation also, and is commonly used when multi-level signals are being employed, whether these arise as combinations of binary signals or directly.

7. Echoes and distortion

Wheeler showed in 1939 that distortion, even when it arises in other ways, can be regarded as due to hypothetical echoes. Attenuation distortion can be interpreted as due to pairs of equal echoes which follow and *precede* the signal by the same time interval; phase distortion implies a pair of echoes in which the echo that follows the signal is reversed. It is often easier to combine these echoes geometrically with a digital signal than to visualize the effects of the corresponding irregularities in the attenuation-frequency and phase-frequency characteristics. It follows that it is practicable to correct for real echoes, and also for attenuation and phase distortion generally, by the calculated introduction of compensating echoes to cancel those disturbing the signal; their generation involves delaying the main signal by a time equal to the longest echo delay. Echo-generating circuits can be made with adjustable controls and used semi-empirically by observing their effect on the received signal's waveform as displayed on an oscilloscope. Used in this way to correct for irregularities in a channel's frequency characteristics they provide a practical example of operating in the 'time domain' to produce an effect in the 'frequency domain'. Signal shaping in the time domain and transmission characteristic equalization in the frequency domain are interchangeable processes.

8. Noise and channel capacity

Shannon showed that the maximum rate, C bits/second, at which information can be transmitted without error over a noisy channel of bandwidth W Hz for a received power of S watts signal and N watts noise is:

$$C = W \log_2 (1 + S/N)$$

In practice this theoretical maximum is an unachievable ideal. For a telephone channel with a bandwidth of 4000 Hz, and a signal-to-noise power ratio of 1000, the formula indicates an information capacity of about 40 000 bits/second, whereas practical channels rarely exceed 5000. No real channel has perfectly equalized characteristics, nor is it practicable or economic to construct the very elaborate coding equipment needed to approach the ideal capacity. The best practical systems need some 4 or 5 times the Shannon power.

9. Error-protecting and error-correcting codes

The first requirement in code protection is to detect the occurrence of an error, and the simplest method adds one extra 'parity bit' to each coded character. Thus, a 7-bit binary code can have an eighth bit added in such a way that each valid code group contains an odd number of 1s. Then a change of any bit from 0 to 1, or vice versa, produces an even number of 1s, which causes the 'parity check' to fail and thus to indicate that an error is present. Such a check is called an 'odd parity check', and it is equally possible to arrange matters so that every valid character contains an even number of 1s in order to provide for an 'even parity check': there is no essential difference between the two methods. A single parity bit cannot detect two changes within one code group—or indeed any even number of changes—but multiple errors within one group are a somewhat less probable event than are single changes. The point, nevertheless, remains, and it is a general one, that the protection given is not absolute; it can do no more than reduce the probability of an error remaining undetected. A more complex method of protective coding uses a code in which of the M bits used in each group to represent a character N are always 1s. Such a code provides for an alphabet of

$$\frac{M!}{N! \, (M - N)!}$$

characters out of the 2^M possible ones if all combinations were to be used. For commercial data a 4-out-of-8 code is common; this provides for 70 characters as compared with the 128 available when the 8-bit groups are used for a 7-bit + parity code, but it also allows some multiple errors to be detected. For example, in one particular trial the number of

errors was halved as compared with a single-parity code; but the result
will depend considerably on the precise nature and distribution of the
noise on the particular channel in use. A 3-out-of-7 code (35 characters)
is used in the popular Van Duuren system for short-wave radio telegraphy.
The parity-bit technique can be extended from an individual character
to a block of a few hundred characters by adding one or more check
characters at the end of the block; these might for example record the
total number of 1s in the block, or for numerical data they might express
the sum of all items or all digits in the block. After reception the count
or summation is repeated and the result compared with the received
check character. In one common form of code the first bit of the check
character is a parity bit for the first bit positions of every character in
the block, the second for the second positions, and so on. Such a check
is called a 'horizontal' or 'longitudional' check—that is, one carried out
along the line of data in contrast to the 'vertical' check of a separate
parity bit for each character. When horizontal and vertical checks are
both used the number of residual errors can easily be reduced by a factor
of 100 or more.

'Casting out the nines' used to be well known as a method of checking
ordinary decimal arithmetic; it depended on observing the remainder
after dividing the numbers involved by nine. In a more general method,
known as a 'modulo-N check', each block of data is treated as a number
that is divided by N and the remainder R is used as a check character.
This approach has been taken further in the 'polynomial' or 'cyclic'
codes which can provide very effective and economical protection
against errors. The method is more complicated to describe than to use,
but suppose a block of data to contain n bits, and let it be represented
by an n-term polynomial:

$$B(x) = a_{n-1}x^{n-1} + a_{n-1}x^{n-2} + \ldots a_1x + a_0$$

in which the coefficients are 0 or 1 according to the corresponding bit
in the block, a_{n-1} being associated with the first bit to be transmitted. A
check character is then formed by using a second 'generating' polynomial
$G(x)$ of order r. $B(x)$ is first multiplied by x^r and then divided by $G(x)$
to leave a remainder $R(x)$ which is the check character for the block. For
example, the use of two 8-bit characters corresponds to a generating
polynomial of the sixteenth order, which might be:

$$G(x) = x^{16} + x^{12} + x^5 + 1$$

The checking procedure is then:
(*a*) add 16 zeros to the end of the block;
(*b*) divide the number so obtained by $G(x)$, that is by the 16-digit
binary number having 1s in positions 16, 12, 5, and 1 and 0s elsewhere,
(*c*) send the 16-bit remainder with the block in the form of two 8-bit
check characters.

Provided the generating polynomial has $(x + 1)$ as a factor, complete
protection is given against any odd number of bit errors, against two
bits in error, and more importantly against groups or bursts of errors r
bits or less in length; and substantial but not complete protection is
given against longer bursts. Many analyses of coding methods have
assumed that each bit is affected independently, that the pattern of noise
disturbance is purely random, but in practice data transmission is more
troubled by impulse noise than by random noise, for when random noise
is low enough to be acceptable for telephony it is too low to bother data
signals; for example, a random noise level high enough to cause a bit error
of 10 per million would be a real nuisance to speech. Impulse noise produces a higher probability of bursts than a purely random distribution
of errors would suggest. This is good in so far as it results in longer periods
of error-free transmission, but bad in that it makes protection more difficult. The protection given by a polynomial code is much greater than
would be given by using the same number of checking bits for vertical
and horizontal parity checks. Nor do the check characters subtract much
from the capacity of the channel: thus, the two 8-bit characters of the
previous example would be suitable for use with blocks of 256 characters
(2048 bits), when they would absorb less than one per cent of the channel
capacity. The price to be paid is not here but in the complexity of the
processes of generation and check, but the electronic equipment is
straightforward, its cost is decreasing rapidly, and the same equipment
can serve for checking as well as for generating.

When an error is detected by any of the preceding methods, the
receiver automatically returns a signal to the sender which triggers it to
re-transmit the faulty block—a procedure known as ARQ. This process
is repeated until the receiver acknowledges the receipt of the block with
no detected error, or for some specified number of times, after which an
alarm is given to the operator. The longer the block the greater will be
the probability that it contains an error, the greater the time wasted in
its re-transmission, and the more costly the equipment needed to store
it temporarily until the receiver confirms that its re-transmission is not
necessary. On the other hand, short blocks employ a higher proportion
of check bits, so wasting more channel capacity. Moreover, the time
lost in turning the channel round—that is, reversing its direction of
transmission—and also in inter-block gaps, absorbs a larger fraction of
the total transmission time. The choice of block length is something of
a compromise and there is a wide variety of lengths in use, ranging from
a single character for slow-speed channels up to 1000 characters for
high-speed channels. The signals returned by the receiver to the sender
require the occasional use of a channel in the reverse direction, but this
channel need not have so wide a band as the main data channel; in a
speech-band link for instance, the forward channel may work at 1200

bits/second and the return at only 75 bits/second. Where the links are short and cost and efficiency are less important, it is economic to provide a full bandwidth channel in each direction, and it is then possible to use a simple 'loop' or 'echo' check in which the received bits are returned to the sender for comparison with those sent, any detected difference halting the process and back-spacing to initiate a re-transmission. Such a system is very secure, but uneconomic in its use of channels.

Re-transmission after the detection of an error is not the only means available to control errors. Codes have been devised which offset the effects of a small number of errors by using a higher degree of redundancy than is needed just to detect errors: in this way they provide 'forward error correction' with no return channel. Clearly, their additional redundancy lowers the efficiency of use of the data channel, and they are not usually attractive for the lower speeds associated with the use of telegraph or telephone channels. Nor, when a return channel is available do they offer better value for money than error-detection and re-transmission because the tariffs charged for two-way channels are little higher than those for unidirectional ones—typically 10 to 30 per cent more. However, forward error correction is attractive for wideband links for the time absorbed in reversed transmission then corresponds to a larger number of data bits lost, and also to more storage at the sending end. The essence of an error-correcting code is that even after say N bits have been corrupted the received character remains more like the sent character than any other in the alphabet. Hamming has analysed these codes in terms of multi-dimensional geometry, and the term 'Hamming distance' is used to indicate the minimum number of elements different between the most similar pairs of characters. A code with a Hamming distance of 2 bits can detect the occurrence of single bit errors, increasing the distance of 3 bits allows single-bit errors to be detected and corrected, a distance of 4 bits can detect double-bit errors or detect and correct single-bit errors, and 5-bit differences permit the forward correction of double-bit errors also.

The polynomial codes mentioned above are intended for use with data in blocks of fixed length, each block being checked independently. It is not, however, necessary to divide the data into blocks, nor always convenient to do so. Hagelbarger and others have devised codes which process a stream of bits continuously and provide forward error correction against bursts: his method separates the check bits associated with a particular group of data bits and interposes an interval sufficiently long to ensure that a burst of the maximum length designed for is not likely to hit more than one bit in the group being checked. To approach the performance indicated by Shannon's formula (see Appendix, § 8) would require the use of very long code words in order to average the noise over as many bits as possible. No method has been found for arriving at the optimum choice of a coding system. Shannon has himself shown that the more nearly a code produces data messages approaching a long random sequence of 0s and 1s (that is, the more nearly it approximates to random noise) the nearer will the probability of errors approach to zero. However, such a code would entail increasingly heavy costs in equipment and in transmission time, for in the limit both tend to infinity.

References

1. LADY LOVELACE, notes to her translation of: *Sketch of the Analytical Engine invented by Charles Babbage Esq.* by L. F. Menabrea; Taylor's Scientific Memoirs, 1843. Reprinted in *Faster than thought,* ed. B. V. Bowden, Pitmans, 1953.
2. SHANNON, C. E. A mathematical theory of communication. *Bell System Technical Journal,* 27, 379 and 623, 1948.
3. BENNET, W. R. and DAVEY, J. R. *Data transmission.* McGraw Hill, 1965.
4. PETERSON, W. W. and WELDON, E. J. *Error correcting codes.* M.I.T. Press, 1972.
5. MARTIN, J. *Teleprocessing network organization.* Prentice Hall, 1969.
6. MATHISON, S. L. and WALKER, P. M. *Computers and telecommunications: Issues in public policy.* Prentice Hall, 1970
7. KIMBEL, D. *Computers and telecommunications-economic, technical and organizational issues.* O.E.C.D. Informatics Study No. 3, Paris 1973.
8. JOHANNESON, OLAF. (Hannes Alvén) *The great computer.* Gollancz, 1968.
9. *Computers and the Year 2000.* National Computing Centre Publications, Manchester, 1972.
10. SACKMAN, H. and NIE, N. (eds) *The information utility and social choice.* American Federation of Information Processing Societies Press, 1970.
11. *Information technology. Some critical implications for decision makers.* The Conference Board, New York, 1972.
12. BUTLER, SAMUEL. *Erewhon.* 1872.

Index

Page numbers in **bold type** indicate definitions or explanations in the text.

Index